A GIFT FOR:

We pray … that you may live a life worthy of the Lord
and may please him in every way:
bearing fruit in every good work, growing in
the knowledge of God, being strengthened with all
power according to his glorious might so that you may
have great endurance and patience.

COLOSSIANS 1:10–11

FROM:

Leadership Secrets of Billy Graham for Graduates
Copyright © 2006 by Christianity Today International
ISBN-10: 0-310-81217-8
ISBN-13: 978-0-310-81217-3

Requests for information should be addressed to:

Inspirio, The gift group of Zondervan
Grand Rapids, Michigan 49530
www.inspiriogifts.com

Compiler: Molly C. Detweiler
Associate Publisher: Tom Dean
Design Manager: Jody Langley
Production Management: Matt Nolan
Design: The DesignWorks Group: cover, Charles Brock; interior, Robin Black
www.thedesignworksgroup.com
Cover Image: Stone Demetrio Carrasco / Getty Images

Printed in China
06 07 08/ 4 3 2 1

LEADERSHIP SECRETS

of BILLY GRAHAM

for GRADUATES

HAROLD MYRA *&*
MARSHALL SHELLEY

inspirio™

CONTENTS

Introduction

PART ONE — COMING ALIVE

1. Igniting! 10
2. The Turning Point 14

PART TWO — GETTING STARTED

3. Forming the Team 22
4. Confronting Temptations 32
5. Lasering in on the Mission 40
6. Loving Harsh Critics 48

PART THREE — CREATING MOMENTUM

7. Communicating Optimism and Hope . . . 58
8. Mobilizing Money 68
9. Empowering Soul Mates 78
10. Expanding the Growing Edge 88

PART FOUR—GROWING THROUGH FIRE & ICE

11. Summoning Courage 98
12. Learning from Failure 108
13. Experiencing Trauma and Betrayal 114
14. Redeeming the Ego 122

PART FIVE—MULTIPLYING MOMENTUM

15. Birthing Dreams 132
16. Building Bridges 140
17. Igniting Other Leaders 150
18. Sowing Seeds in All Seasons 160

PART SIX—DEEPENING IN EVERY DECADE

19. Learning—and Leveraging Weakness . . 170
20. Plugging into Continuous Voltage 180
21. Innovating 190
22. Leading with Love 198

INTRODUCTION

When you hear the name *Billy Graham,* do you think first of his leadership? Most of us do not. We recall his preaching to vast crowds in stadiums. We remember his leading the nation in dramatic times of grief, or helping inaugurate presidents, but more as national pastor than leader.

Yet Billy begins his autobiography by saying, "My responsibilities as chief executive officer of the Billy Graham Evangelistic Association have always demanded a tremendous amount of time and decision making."

I contacted Billy about writing a book to help convey the principles of his leadership. When I received a letter back from him, I blinked and then smiled as I read it:

"It seems to me that the Lord took several inexperienced young men and used them in ways they never dreamed," Billy wrote. "The ministry sort of took off and got away from all of us! We all seemed to be a part of a tremendous movement of the Spirit of God, and so many of the new organizations seemed to interrelate, or began as we talked and prayed together on our travels. It was natural to encourage and help them along."

Billy always insists on simply being called "Billy." He titled his autobiography *Just As I Am,* a perfect description of his humble spirit, taken from the hymn sung when he invites people to come forward and receive God's love. With humble audacity and "ferocious resolve," Billy has led with full, even painful, awareness of his own strengths and limitations.

Those of us called to some sort of leadership realize that "just as I am" describes each of us as we face demanding, complex challenges. In the refining furnace of leadership, we sense we must seek empowerment from above. And we know we simply must do the best we can with what we have and who we are.

Billy Graham did that. Whatever the challenges and hurdles, whatever the limitations, he steadily led by full commitment to his biblical values. His lifetime of vigorous leadership invites us to engage with the same spirit, to consider his examples, and to reach, as he did, into the rich resources of leadership literature that resonate with scriptural principles.

Harold Myra

Part One

Coming Alive

H*ow is it that among millions
of young people of no particular
distinction, one ignites and
becomes a driving force?
How is it that—like a rocket
on a launchpad with flame
barely visible—one person is
slightly lifted, then slowly gains
momentum, thrusts upward,
engines burning steadily with
increasing velocity?*

IGNITING!

[Jesus] will ignite the kingdom life, a fire,
the Holy Spirit within you,
changing you from the inside out.
LUKE 3:16 THE MESSAGE

Leadership is forged in the furnace. Far from being a
formula to learn, leadership is a set of life
experiences melded by intense heat.

Billy Graham's lifetime of leadership has, indeed,
been a blending of extraordinary humility with fierce
intensity of purpose.

All this from a skinny farm kid from Charlotte,
North Carolina? What ignited all this? Who could have
come anywhere close to predicting it?

Not his grade school teachers!

His fifth-grade teacher said, "I just couldn't get him
to say a word in class. I remember once, he just sat there
looking at me after I asked him a question, and I finally
burst out in exasperation, 'Billy Frank, don't just sit
there—say something. Please, just say *something*.' Not a
sound. He just kept staring at me. And to tell you the
truth, I just forgot about him after he passed on out of
school. Then, I don't know how many years later, I saw

him for the first time on one of his television crusades. I simply couldn't believe it. His whole personality was so completely changed. He had such certainty, and the way the words were just pouring out—I kept thinking, somebody's putting the words in his mouth, he's just pantomiming it out. I couldn't get over it. I kept thinking, Is that actually Billy Frank Graham? What in the world happened to him?"

What in the world *did* happen to Billy Frank Graham?

These [difficulties] have come so that your faith—
of greater worth than gold, which perishes even
though refined by fire—may be proved
genuine and may result in praise,
glory and honor when Jesus Christ
is revealed.

1 Peter 1:7

Immersion in the furnace of leadership formation began with a painful experience with a beautiful young woman. Emily Cavanaugh was a dark-haired college classmate whom Billy had asked to marry him. But Emily said, "I'm not sure we're right for each other. I just don't see any real purpose in your life yet." Billy was devastated. For months afterward, he felt "a tremendous burden." He didn't, in fact, have a sense of purpose.

After months of angst, one autumn evening, he gazed upward and cried out to God. "All right, Lord! If you want me, you've got me," Billy declared. "If I'm never to get Emily, I'm gonna follow you. No girl or anything else will come first in my life again. You can have all of me from now on. I'm gonna follow you at all cost."

Whom have I in heaven but you?
And earth has nothing I desire besides you.
PSALM 73:25

Billy's soul was ablaze. He was full of passion to fulfill what he believed God was calling him to—spreading the gospel, "the Good News," as a message of liberation and love.

THE TURNING POINT

Billy's next step toward his God-given purpose would come during a mission to the British Isles. There he met a young Welsh evangelist named Stephen Olford, who had the spiritual qualities Billy longed for. After hearing Olford preach on being filled with the Holy Spirit, Billy approached him and said, "You've spoken of something that I don't have. I want the fullness of the Holy Spirit in my life, too."

"I can still hear Billy pouring out his heart in a prayer of total dedication to the Lord," said Olford. "Finally, he said, 'My heart is so flooded with the Holy Spirit!' and we went from praying to praising. We were laughing and praising God, and Billy was walking back and forth across the room, crying out, 'I have it! I'm filled. This is a turning point in my life.' And he was a new man."

That night, when Billy preached, "for reasons known to God alone, the place which was only moderately filled the night before was packed to the doors," said Olford. "As Billy rose to speak, he was a man absolutely anointed."

Members of the audience came forward to pray even before Billy gave an invitation. At the end of the sermon, practically the entire crowd rushed forward.

"My own heart was so moved by Billy's authority and strength that I could hardly drive home," Olford remembers. "When I came in the door, my father looked at my face and said, 'What on earth happened?' I sat down at the kitchen table and said, 'Dad, something has happened to Billy Graham. The world is going to hear from this man.'"

*May the God of hope fill you with all joy and peace
as you trust in him, so that you may overflow
with hope by the power of the Holy Spirit.*

ROMANS 15:13

THE GIANTS ALL HAD ONE THING
IN COMMON: NEITHER VICTORY NOR
SUCCESS, BUT PASSION.

Philip Yancey

*[Jesus said,] "You will receive power when the
Holy Spirit comes on you; and you will
be my witnesses in Jerusalem, and in all Judea and
Samaria, and to the ends of the earth."*

ACTS 1:8

*I am not ashamed of the gospel,
because it is the power of God for the salvation
of everyone who believes.*

ROMANS 1:16

Sherwood Wirt, longtime editor of Billy's *Decision* magazine, observed, "All attempts to explain Billy Graham fail unless they begin at the cross."

What did he mean by that? Billy read often in the Bible the words of Jesus to his disciples, "Whoever desires to come after me, let him deny himself, and take up his cross, and follow me. For whoever desires to save his life will lose it, but whoever loses his life for my sake and the gospel's will save it." Billy denied himself in countless ways and took up his cross—and followed Jesus.

Christians believe that the salvation of a single soul is of supreme value; all else fades beside this greatest consideration—that each person will live forever, either separated from God, or blessedly and joyfully in community with him. Billy knew the Bible stated Jesus had suffered the horrors of the cross "for the joy that was set before him." He, too, was fueled by that proffered joy.

The principles of Billy's remarkable blending of humility and intense resolve are gifts anyone can seek. We see the necessity of the burning purpose … and the humility to balance it out. To grow throughout your lifetime, as Billy has, is a lifelong quest.

Art and education may refine the taste, but they cannot purify the heart and regenerate the individual. His [Christ's] words were simple yet profound. And they shook people, provoking either happy acceptance or violent rejection. People were never the same after listening to Him.... The people who followed Him were unique in their generation. They turned the world upside down because their hearts had been turned right side up. The world has never been the same.

Billy Graham

*Let us fix our eyes on Jesus, the author and perfecter
of our faith, who for the joy set before him
endured the cross, scorning its shame, and sat down
at the right hand of the throne of God.*

Hebrews 12:2

*God was pleased to have all his fullness dwell
in [Christ], and through him to reconcile to himself all
things, whether things on earth or things in heaven,
by making peace through his blood, shed on the cross.
Once you were alienated from God and were enemies
in your minds because of your evil behavior.
But now he has reconciled you by Christ's physical body
through death to present you holy in his sight,
without blemish and free from accusation.*

Colossians 1:19–22

*May I never boast except in the cross of our
Lord Jesus Christ, through which the world has been
crucified to me, and I to the world.*

Galatians 6:14

GETTING STARTED

While still in his twenties, Billy Graham became nationally known. With his team he laid the foundations for decades of international ministry. What set him apart from so many other young men of the period?

How did he form a core team that lasted a lifetime? What factors helped bring him such tremendous success?

FORMING THE TEAM

Jesus went up on a mountainside and called to him those he wanted, and they came to him. He appointed twelve—designating them apostles—that they might be with him and that he might send them out to preach.

MARK 3:13–14

It seems to me that the Lord took several inexperienced young men and used them in ways they never dreamed." This is how Billy describes the founding of his core team—a team that has now been together for more than 50 years.

His instinct is to immediately defer credit to God and to that team. "The ministry sort of took off and got away from all of us! We all seemed to be a part of a tremendous movement of the Spirit of God."

Before he was led to build his own ministry team, Billy got some on-the-job training as the first full-time employee of Youth for Christ. As a part of YFC Billy traveled constantly, meeting with pastors, YFC directors, and other leaders. Through these experiences, Billy saw what it took to build long-lasting, solid teams.

Energetic entrepreneurship drove the movement forward, but the nature of its passion made the results far different from those in the business world. Youth For Christ leaders believed they were dependent on the Holy Spirit, who could do the only truly valuable work. Hundreds of leaders would pray together long into the night, kneeling on auditorium floors. They would confess sinful attitudes to each other and ask for God's cleansing and empowerment. Together they poured over the Bible. Out of that brash, driven, try-anything culture came a spirit of *teamwork*.

So before his own team was formed, Billy spent years in the ministry trenches, deepening his convictions, refining his strategies, and sensing who could be his own ministry soul mates.

Slowly, Billy began recruiting his own team as the Lord led him to those soul mates. Then, they set out together on their mission to spread the Good News. They faced large challenges together. They were amazed, stretched, deepened, enriched—together.

I thank my God every time I remember you.
In all my prayers for all of you,
I always pray with joy because of your partnership in
the gospel from the first day until now.

Philippians 1:3–5

Billy's team members saw the larger picture, and when Billy Graham spoke of his dreams, the dreams were theirs as well. Strong team members have strong egos, and playing second fiddle can feel unnatural. But team players know the greatest glory is the entire team's victory.

Leadership always comes with a price. A team understands that each player contributes, each has burdens to bear and challenges to confront, and each must follow.

Billy found the balance of both leading and following. He led his ministry's board … but also sought their accountability as protection and as a source of wisdom.

The essential part of this balance, though, was that Billy was constantly asking the question, "What is God actually saying we should do next?" … He was a highly effective leader with clarity of purpose because he was determined that nothing would short-circuit his responding to the nudges of the Holy Spirit.

[Jesus said,] "Whoever wants to become great among you must be your servant, and whoever wants to be first must be your slave—just as the Son of Man did not come to be served, but to serve, and to give his life as a ransom for many."

MATTHEW 20:26–28

Whoever exalts himself will be humbled, and whoever humbles himself will be exalted.

MATTHEW 23:12

[Jesus said,] "I have set you an example that you should do as I have done for you. I tell you the truth, no servant is greater than his master, nor is a messenger greater than the one who sent him. Now that you know these things, you will be blessed if you do them."

JOHN 13:15–17

TEAMBUILDING

APPLYING THE PRINCIPLES

How can we apply Billy's approach to teambuilding when we have opportunities to lead? We can't always choose our leaders or our teammates, … but whatever our … opportunities and limitations, the spirit of teambuilding empowers and energizes.

USE ASTOUNDING MATH

Whether you are leading a small or large group, teamwork multiplies effectiveness. When members of a team use their special strengths and are passionate about the goal, "mountains can be moved." Building a team is a tall challenge. We must be realistic about the difficulties and make adjustments as necessary. But when we truly work together we are often amazed at the results.

Two are better than one,
because they have a good return for their work.
ECCLESIASTES 4:9

WATCH OUT! CHEMISTRY CAN EMPOWER, OR EXPLODE

A positive blending of personality and temperament is one of the top factors in building a great team. The mix of chemistry must include loyalty, trust, respect, and a deep sense of shared goals. When we have the opportunity to select team members, we must listen to our intuitions and best counselors. Working with soul mates lifts any enterprise or ministry.

"BILLY IS A FRIEND OF THE TEAM.
HE SPOKE OF THE TEAM AND TEAM ACTIVITIES AS
'OURS,' NOT AS 'ME AND MINE.'...
HE RESPECTED THE GIFTS GOD GAVE US. ...
HE TRUSTED THE LORD AND THE CHOICES HE
MADE OF LEADERS.
AS A RESULT, WE WOULD HAVE — AND DID —
FOLLOW HIM ANYWHERE GOD LED.
WE WOULD EVEN HAVE LAID DOWN
OUR LIVES FOR HIM."

*Cliff Barrows, member of Billy's ministry team
for over fifty years*

Face, and Admit, Your Own Limitations

Authenticity—being "real"—and love … create and energize teams for the long haul. Grady Wilson said of Billy, "He was painfully aware of his humanity—he has flaws, and he's the first to admit them." Billy didn't try to hide what he couldn't do. His vulnerability and style of working side by side made his team well aware of both his strengths and his weaknesses.

Take Time to Laugh

Teams that emphasize fun and good spirits lift effectiveness.

Billy would tell stories on himself. For instance, he liked to tell of the time in a small town when he asked a boy how to get to the post office. After getting directions, Billy invited him to come to the meeting that evening. "You can hear me telling everyone how to get to heaven."

The boy's response? "I don't think I'll be there. You don't even know your way to the post office."

A cheerful heart is good medicine.
PROVERBS 17:22

Communicate a Clear Goal to Pursue Together

Large challenges energize and coalesce teams. In sports, preparing for the Super Bowl or World Series has an amazing effect on concentration, energy, and determination. Every player is fully psyched to achieve the goal and will do whatever possible to win. In many cases, individual preferences and chances for personal glory must be shoved aside for the full-court press toward victory….Urgency, direction, mutual accountability, and respect all blend as everyone on the team determines to seek the highest performance possible.

Blend Your Principles and Personalities

Over time a good team works increasingly well together because they can anticipate one another's reactions and handle the inevitable surprises in a coordinated way. Healthy teams share both a common mission and a common bond.

> Let us hold unswervingly to the hope we profess, for he who promised is faithful. And let us consider how we may spur one another on toward love and good deeds.
>
> Hebrews 10:23–24

Place Confidence in the Team

The leader's attitude toward the team largely determines how strong it will become. The Graham team became strong because Billy nourished it and gave each member ample opportunity to exercise significant responsibility.

> "Billy was confident in God. He sought God's will....He knew in the multitude of counselors there is safety. His decisions were based on mutual agreement....He...relied on the counsel of those he trusted."
>
> *Cliff Barrows*

When Your Team Is Finally All Set, Expect Change!

We must accept the fact that powerful, complex forces make change inevitable. Dealing effectively and compassionately with painful changes requires continuing focus on the vision and goal, and consistency with your principles. In today's world, leaders must face the fact that change is accelerating at numbing speed, and that keeping a team together—or reconfiguring it—can require lots of adaptations to new realities.

CONFRONTING
TEMPTATIONS

[Jesus said,] "Watch and pray so that you
will not fall into temptation.
The spirit is willing, but the body is weak."

MARK 14:38

When Billy Graham was shaping his leadership principles and commitments, many of the temptations were, perhaps, less overt, less "in-your-face" than they are today. Yet the power of the temptations was not any less, and they were in essence the same ones we face now.

Billy saw how spiritual enthusiasm did not make you immune to greed, pride, lust, and ambition. Indeed, spiritual passion and more earthly passions often possess the same soul.

Billy carefully observed other traveling preachers during his own early ministry and learned from the mistakes he witnessed many of them make. Wrote historian George Marsden, "Seeing the terrible disillusionment trusting church folks had suffered due to the failures of preachers stirred deep revulsion within him and added an increasingly dogged determination to adhere to high standards of morality and ethics."

Just a few years later, in 1948, this determination led to a fateful afternoon discussion with his newly formed evangelistic team. It would chart the course his ministry would take for the next half century.

Righteousness guards the man of integrity.
PROVERBS 13:6

I know, my God, that you test the heart
and are pleased with integrity.
1 CHRONICLES 29:17

Because [Christ] himself suffered when he was tempted,
he is able to help those who are being tempted.
HEBREWS 2:18

The man of integrity walks securely,
but he who takes crooked paths will be found out.
PROVERBS 10:9

No temptation has seized you except what is common
to man. And God is faithful; he will not
let you be tempted beyond what you can bear.
But when you are tempted, he will also provide a way
out so that you can stand up under it.
1 CORINTHIANS 10:13

One afternoon during evangelistic meetings in Modesto, California, Billy called the team together to discuss how they might guard themselves against the failures so many other ministries had faced.

"God has brought us to this point," he said. "Maybe he is preparing us for something that we don't know. Let's try to recall all the things that have been a stumbling block and a hindrance to evangelists in years past, and let's come back together in an hour and talk about it and pray about it and ask God to guard us from them.

"When they returned," Billy remembers, "the lists were remarkably similar, and we soon made a series of resolutions that would guide us in our future evangelistic work. It was a shared commitment to do all we could to uphold the Bible's standard of absolute integrity and purity for evangelists."

Out of this discussion, Billy's team developed guidelines that they would follow for the rest of their lives. It came to be known as "The Modesto Manifesto."

Their discussion boiled down to four main points:

Avoid shady handling of money—"We determined to do all we could to avoid financial abuses and to downplay the offering and depend as much as possible on money raised by local communities in advance."

Avoid even the appearance of sexual immorality— "We pledged among ourselves to avoid any situation that would have even the appearance of compromise or suspicion. From that day on I did not travel, meet, or eat alone with a woman other than my wife."

Avoid badmouthing others doing similar work— The team recognized that while it's often easier in the short-term to operate independently, it's better in the long run to work with others. Billy said, "We were determined …to avoid an antichurch or anticlergy attitude."

Avoid exaggerating accomplishments—Credibility is a precious commodity. The Graham team determined to avoid any appearance of padding the numbers of those attending their events.

Billy's team structured the ministry to reinforce guidelines and hold themselves accountable. Cliff Barrows told us, "We were accountable to God, to our wives, to each other, the local committees, and the spiritual leadership of the community."

Whatever is true, whatever is noble, whatever is right,
whatever is pure, whatever is lovely,
whatever is admirable—if anything is excellent
or praiseworthy—think about such things.

Philippians 4:8

TEMPTATIONS

APPLYING THE PRINCIPLES

Talent can take you far, but the accomplishments that talent brings also produce great temptations. How do we build the will and the strength of character to confront and overcome temptations? Here are a few lessons we can use from Billy Graham's approach to temptation:

NEVER UNDERESTIMATE A "SMALL TEMPTATION"

Temptation can blindside you. A small white lie appears worth the risk. But only after we give in to a temptation do we discover its strength.

> REPUTATIONS ARE FRAGILE.
> THEY MUST BE HANDLED WITH CARE LIKE A
> VALUABLE VASE THAT IF DROPPED
> CAN NEVER QUITE BE PUT TOGETHER AGAIN.
>
> *Bill Pollard*

Minimize Secrecy; Maximize Reinforcements

When we minimize secrecy and openly admit temptations are there, we can build in safeguards against poor judgment, unconscious motivations, and self-deception. A great defense against falling into temptation is discussing the temptations you face with others, and then working together to set guidelines that will protect you.

Practice Open Integrity

If you determine to always be open and honest, no matter what, you will diffuse the power of many temptations. Don't just avoid outright lies; avoid exaggerating the truth as well. Make it hard for anyone to find any "dirt" on you.

Set Your Eyes on the Larger Prize

We all know that concentrating on overcoming a temptation often has the ironic effect of making it stronger. In contrast, focusing on something powerful and positive empowers mind and emotions to embrace God's best. When you're faced with a temptation, turn it off by focusing on God's great plan for you.

We all struggle with temptations, even though they are different for each of us. But when we allow ourselves to be caught up in something larger than ourselves, we find temptations losing their power over us.

LASERING IN
ON THE MISSION

*Forgetting what is behind and straining toward
what is ahead, I press on toward the goal
to win the prize for which God has called me
heavenward in Christ Jesus.*

PHILIPPIANS 3:13–14

A laser so focuses the power of light that it can slice steel or perform surgery. While broad exposure and wide-ranging interests are important, leaders who offer the most lasting contributions incorporate their exposure into a laser focus. Without a clear purpose, your energy is scattered and your power is lessened.

The great evangelist of the nineteenth century, Dwight L. Moody, who in many ways was a model for Billy Graham, had a motto: "Consecrate, then concentrate." Billy did just that. He identified his calling, then refused to be diverted.

For Billy, as for almost every effective leader, distractions and potential diversions continually confronted him.

Early in his career, Billy's charisma and good looks led to an offer from Paramount Pictures Corporation to become an actor. He declined. In the late 1950s, NBC offered him one million dollars a year to host a show. He turned it down. President Richard Nixon offered him an ambassadorship, a cabinet post, "any job I wanted." A Texas billionaire offered Billy six million dollars if he would run for president.

As attractive as these options may have been, Billy realized they were not part of his mission. To each he said, "God called me to preach, and I do not intend to do anything else as long as I live." Billy's focus was clear.

Telling the Good News of salvation to everyone he met was, and remains, Billy's primary mission in life. Not only did he refuse to be distracted by money and fame, he also chose not to be distracted by the many political causes and movements that have arisen during the years he's been in ministry.

John Akers, one of Billy's closest aides, told us, "Billy's principle was that you shouldn't do anything that would shut the door to the gospel. I can't tell you how important that is. People are constantly wanting him to sign a petition about something, and he declines. He's been called a moral coward for not taking this stand, or that stand, or the other stand. But from his standpoint, to do so was to unnecessarily close doors to the gospel."

Another important aspect of Billy's focus was his ability to recognize his own role and to stick to it. Billy focused on one element—connecting with broad audiences and bringing them to the point of decision. That means he primarily leaves to others the task of helping people grow in faith.

Billy lasers in on explaining the decision a person needs to make regarding Jesus. When a person makes that decision, Billy encourages local churches to follow up with them and encourage their spiritual growth.

Billy knows what his God-given gifts are and focuses on using them well. He also realizes what gifts he *doesn't* have and allows others to take over in their areas of giftedness.

There are different kinds of gifts,
but the same Spirit.
There are different kinds of service,
but the same Lord.
There are different kinds of working,
but the same God works all of them in all men.
Now to each one the manifestation
of the Spirit is given for the common good.

1 Corinthians 12:4–7

Billy was so focused on bringing his message to every venue that he would somehow always find a way to do it. His use of the microphone check illustrates the intensity of his focus.

A. Larry Ross, media relations director for Billy, told this story: "Almost always before a TV interview, they do a microphone check, and they ask the interviewee to say something—anything—so they can adjust the audio settings. Often a corporate executive, for that check, will count to ten, say his ABCs, or recite what he had for breakfast. Mr. Graham would always quote John 3:16.

When I asked Mr. Graham why he does that, he replied, 'Because that way, if I am not able to communicate the gospel clearly during the interview, at least the cameraman will have heard it.'"

Let your eyes look straight ahead,
   fix your gaze directly before you.
Make level paths for your feet
   and take only ways that are firm.
Do not swerve to the right or the left;
   keep your foot from evil.

PROVERBS 4:25–27

BE SURE YOU PUT YOUR FEET
IN THE RIGHT PLACE,
AND THEN STAND FIRM.

Author Unknown

A man of understanding keeps a straight course.

PROVERBS 15:21

"GIVE ME A MAN WHO SAYS,
'THIS ONE THING I DO,'
NOT 'THESE FIFTY I DABBLE IN.'"

Dwight L. Moody

LASERING

APPLYING THE PRINCIPLES

To be a good leader you must identify the essential goal and continually move toward it. As someone put it, "If you chase two rabbits, both will escape." A leader who identifies one unifying principle and bases all decisions on that is more likely to achieve "greatness" than a leader who does many things.

IDENTIFY THE ONE THING

Work hard to discover your calling and then stick to it. Billy was a prime example of a leader with a one-point agenda. "I used to talk on every subject," he admitted. "If somebody asked me anything political, I'd talk on it. I've learned through the years that I'm much better off keeping quiet on certain subjects in order that I may appeal to a wider group of people in my presentation of the gospel."

DON'T HUNT RABBITS

When you're looking to bag a great big buck, you don't go hunting rabbits! And when you're pursuing your mission, you must guard against getting distracted by little things. For instance, Billy let his hair grow a little longer in the 1970s to identify with the younger generation. Billy said, "It's ridiculous for parents to engage in bitter battles with their children over the haircut issue…long hair or short hair is a matter of personal taste, not a basic moral question." Billy didn't want to be diverted by secondary targets.

Cast the Vision; Ask for Big Things

In addition to keeping the vision uncluttered, a leader must recognize what limits its fulfillment, and that may require asking for help. Billy realized that he needed help early in his ministry with one-on-one counseling for the people who came forward to make decisions for Christ at his meetings. With the help they received, Billy could give himself fully to his mission, which was preaching, knowing that the people's needs were still being met.

Broaden Your Base of Help

Because Billy was clear about his primary mission, he could welcome help from others, even from some who differed on other issues. This has been the source of some of the most vocal criticism of Billy Graham over the years. But Billy's clarity of focus allowed him to keep relationships in perspective, and to make allies out of sometimes unlikely people, all for the sake of the gospel.

Maximize Mission Clarity

Infecting others with a sense of urgency is the difference between effective and ineffective leaders. Billy's pattern was to devote himself to the urgency of his cause with a lifetime of persistence. His passion radiated to others who in turn joined him in his sense of urgency and persistence for the gospel.

> Throughout history,
> it was the super achievers —
> and only the super achievers —
> who knew when to say "No."
> They always knew what to
> reach for. They knew
> where to place themselves.
>
> *Peter Drucker*

LOVING HARSH CRITICS

All leaders get criticized. It's their response to criticism that sets them apart. Our natural reactions to criticism include emotions ranging from woundedness and indignation to desire for revenge. Today our culture conditions us to amplify our reactive emotions, to use our verbal weapons against others. This constant undercurrent flowing into our subconscious affects us more than we may realize.

The strategy of Billy Graham has been the polar opposite of this dark undercurrent. To even his harshest critics he genuinely reached out in love, thereby redeeming many a volatile situation but also empowering his own soul.

Did Billy get angry with his critics? Of course he did. Billy may be viewed by many as all sweetness and light, but his life and spirit are the results of gritty determination to love God, to lead from that love, and to forgive, and even learn from, his "enemies."

Billy's response to his critics, for the most part, was to simply brush off their disapproval. He feared engaging them would ultimately detract from his mission. "Satan would like nothing better than to have us stop our ministry and start answering critics, tracking down wretched lies and malicious stories," he said of his policy in 1952. "By God's grace I shall continue to preach the gospel of Jesus Christ and not stoop to mudslinging, name-calling, and petty little fights over nonessentials."

Whenever possible, Billy used love to diffuse criticism and, sometimes, even make friends of his harshest critics.

During a preaching campaign in Birmingham, England, in 1947, Billy had faced intense opposition from skeptical local pastors. Through the years itinerant revival preachers had passed through Birmingham and drummed up local support by denouncing the local clergy. So before Billy even arrived, these pastors, sure that he was just another religious opportunist, convinced the city council to prohibit him from speaking in the city auditorium.

When Billy showed up, he didn't grouse about this prohibition. Instead, he made appointments with his detractors, one by one, admitted his weaknesses as a young preacher, and assured them he wanted only to help them reach the city for Christ. He asked them calmly to explain and pray about their opposition. Soon the hostility morphed into fervent support.

BILLY'S APPROACH TO HANDLING CRITICISM
WAS TO "GO DIRECTLY TO THE PEOPLE
CAUSING HIM THE MOST PAIN
AND BASICALLY SAY, "TEACH ME."

*Lon Allison, director of the Billy Graham
Center at Wheaton College*

One of the hardest lessons to learn is how to take criticism well. But when you find the strength to learn and grow from even your harshest critics, you'll find yourself becoming a much stronger person than you ever were before.

Endure hardship as discipline;
God is treating you as sons.
HEBREWS 12:7

[Jesus said,] "Blessed are you when people insult you,
persecute you and falsely say all kinds of evil against
you because of me. Rejoice and be glad, because great is
your reward in heaven, for in the same way they
persecuted the prophets who were before you."
MATTHEW 5:11–12

CRITICS

APPLYING THE PRINCIPLES

All of us need all the insights we can get about ourselves and our challenges, and if we look at our critics as sources of insight, we can leverage even painful and mean-spirited critiques. Critics can sharpen the mind and clarify parameters. They can force us to evaluate what we really believe about ourselves and our mission. How we respond to critics reveals a lot about our sense of calling and our composure.

EXPECT TO BE CRITICIZED

Leadership, by definition, means change, which makes criticism inevitable. When criticism is a threat, a leader becomes defensive, but when it is viewed as a natural occurrence and a challenge, it can become a source of constructive energy.

BE REALISTIC ABOUT OUR DUAL NATURES

Even the best people are still inhabited by an "old self," as the Bible describes it. We should never be caught by surprise at people's negative behavior but accept it as a reminder that our work as leaders is not done.

A wise older pastor once observed, "The qualifications of a pastor are to have the mind of a scholar, the heart of a child, and the hide of a rhinoceros." That's true of any leader as well. Especially the part about the hide.

EMBRACE THREE ESSENTIALS

Settle on your deepest convictions about your mission—Know what you believe and what you will not compromise.

Ignore most criticism—Don't let a criticism bother you so much that it distracts you from your purpose. It's helpful to have a friend or two who can help you sort the criticisms to ignore from the ones to be carefully considered.

Don't respond reactively—Billy frequently took several days before responding to criticisms. He knew the importance of avoiding a knee-jerk reaction. At times he didn't respond at all, especially when critics ridiculed him personally or attacked his motives. "He could never answer those criticisms, for he told me that trying to answer those kinds of charges drained him of his energy," said Cliff Barrows.

"Billy had a practice never to speak disparagingly of another person publicly," said Cliff Barrows. He recalled a situation … when a local pastor's members were very involved in a campaign, but the pastor felt the meetings were hindering his church ministry, infringing on the Wednesday night prayer services.

"For eight weeks, this pastor called Billy personally to complain that his work was being hindered, and that Billy didn't care about local churches," recalled Cliff. "Billy told him we were trying to follow the Lord's leading, and that he wanted to encourage his church members, not hinder them. The congregation told the pastor they wanted to promote the meetings and be part of them, but they sensed his hostility.

"On the last weekend, Billy called him and said, 'Sir, I want to thank you for the leadership your church has provided in this series of meetings, and you would do me a great honor to sit with me on the platform. I'd like to introduce you and ask you to lead in prayer.' The pastor was overwhelmed."

Sometimes the best way to get rid of a critic is to turn him into a friend. Through a grace-filled and humble response, leaders can sometimes do that.

ACCEPT THE GIFT OF A GOOD ENEMY

"Without my enemies," a person of high achievement says, "I would never have been challenged to reach the next level, never would have found the determination to excel." Sometimes we need enemies to press us to new heights, just as a football team needs a challenging opponent to drive them to extraordinary effort.

When a man's ways are pleasing to the LORD,
he makes even his enemies live at peace with him.

PROVERBS 16:7

[Jesus said,] "You have heard that it was said,
'Love your neighbor and hate your enemy.'
But I tell you: Love your enemies and
pray for those who persecute you, that you may be
sons of your Father in heaven."

MATTHEW 5:43–45

Love your enemies, do good to them,
and lend to them without expecting to get anything
back. Then your reward will be great.

LUKE 6:35

PART THREE

CREATING
MOMENTUM

Billy turns out to be very human, like the rest of us, but with a powerful intuitive grasp of what's required to lead effectively.

He has been able to overcome his own personal tendencies toward pessimism, delegate intelligently those things that were not his strengths, lead and energize others in spite of the pressures of the spotlight, and through it all, continue to grow and change as the times called for it.

COMMUNICATING
OPTIMISM AND HOPE

Blessed is the man who finds wisdom,
the man who gains understanding,
for she is more profitable than silver
and yields better returns than gold.
PROVERBS 3:13–14

Longer than anyone else, decade after decade after decade, Billy Graham has been included in *Good Housekeeping*'s most-admired list. Over the years, presidents and other luminaries have appeared, then faded. But Billy has always been at or near the top of the list.

One day Fred Smith, who had chaired one of Billy's Cincinnati crusades, asked us, "Have you thought about the *Good Housekeeping* list?"

"Not particularly."

"Take a close look. Every person on it is *positive*."

But here is a remarkable thing we learned. His family nicknamed him Puddleglum. Puddleglum is a brave but glum creature from C.S Lewis' *Chronicles of Narnia* stories who is always expecting the worst."

Billy's family uses the nickname for him with humor and affection, but how could it really fit? Most of us, sensing a rightness about Billy's being chosen most admired and often being called "the beloved evangelist," would never dream of his being nicknamed Puddleglum. His family and closest friends saw a side the public did not—a dubious, pessimistic tendency that he had to fight constantly.

But despite the worst, Billy knew that a leader must personify hope for the best.

The optimistic, thoughtful leader is well aware of the brutal realities, the questions, the what-ifs. The leader may feel jangled nerves but *chooses* the way of faith and hope, knowing he must communicate that to others.

Be strong and take heart,
all you who hope in the LORD.

PSALM 31:24

The LORD delights in those who fear him,
who put their hope in his unfailing love.

PSALM 147:11

We also rejoice in our sufferings, because we know that
suffering produces perseverance; perseverance, character;
and character, hope. And hope does not disappoint us,
because God has poured out his love into
our hearts by the Holy Spirit, whom he has given us.

ROMANS 5:3–5

Billy Graham endured attacks, rough-and-tumble opposition, and lots of reversals. Did this make him despondent?

At times, yes, but Billy's associates also speak of his "undiluted enthusiasm" and his "constant air of expectancy." He has always been eager to learn and to move on to the next challenge. At the same time, Billy carried his heavy responsibilities with extreme seriousness.

One thing is clear. Billy Graham has plenty of reasons to see life's downsides. As a perceptive human being, he feels his vulnerable position in the public eye, and he can foresee possible backlashes from his decisions and actions. The pressures on him affect him physically. But he has determined to live by his convictions and the gospel of hope, and to communicate that confidence to others.

OPTIMISM

APPLYING THE PRINCIPLES

Optimism is not living in a fantasy world where nothing tragic ever happens; vital optimism is a confidence that tragedy is not the last word, that the best is yet to be. Optimism is being able to acknowledge brutal realities and to point to an even greater reality—that our experiences are not in vain, our responses are not futile, and our efforts are going to be worthwhile. Sometimes bringing hope to a dispirited group is the most important thing a leader can do.

> WHATEVER ENLARGES HOPE
> WILL ALSO EXALT COURAGE.
> *Samuel Johnson*

> IF YOU DO NOT HOPE YOU WILL NEVER
> DISCOVER WHAT IS BEYOND YOUR HOPES.
> *Clement of Alexandria*

Respond with the Math of Hope

In Mother Teresa's India, the hopeless and the dying are like an endless sea of despair. Someone asked her how, considering this enormity, she could continue day after day, year after year with her ministry to the dying. She responded that looking at it that way applied the wrong math. She used *subtraction*. Every time she loved and cared for a destitute and dying man, every time she rescued a girl from prostitution, she was subtracting from the despair and adding to hope.

The following story by author and scientist Loren Eiseley is a beautiful example of facing overwhelming odds with overwhelming hope.

The Star Thrower

On a beach in Costabel, Eiseley saw great numbers of empty shells, "the debris of life." He watched gulls cut a hermit crab to pieces and wrote, "Death walks hugely and in many forms."

One dawn, he surveyed what the night's ocean had deposited. "Long-limbed starfish were strewn everywhere." Eiseley knew the tiny breathing pores of the starfish were stuffed with sand, and the rising sun would shrivel their bodies.

Rounding a bluff, he discerned the star thrower.

It was a man who stooped to pick up a starfish, then loft it far out to sea. Eiseley approached him. "It may live," the man said of the starfish, "if the off-shore pull is strong enough."

The man stooped again and threw another starfish back to its natural habitat. "The stars," he said, "throw well. One can help them."

Eiseley saw in the man's skimming the starfish out into the water "the posture of a god." Yet he also wrote, "The star thrower is a man, and death is running more fleet than he along every sea beach in the world."

Despite that fact, the star thrower kept at his task. "One can help them," he reasoned.

Does death win it all? Is life meaningless? Or is there hope? Each of us must choose the math of subtraction—of reducing despair—or the math of being overwhelmed and sinking into cynicism.

EVERYTHING THAT IS DONE
IN THE WORLD IS DONE BY HOPE.

Martin Luther

Stay on the Horse

> THERE ARE SO MANY BATTLES WON
> OR LOST DEPENDING ON WHETHER THE
> PEOPLE INVOLVED HANG ON JUST A LITTLE
> BIT LONGER. SO THE LEADER HAS A PRIMARY
> OBLIGATION NOT TO DECLARE DOUBTS
> OR FAILURES AT THE DROP OF A HAT.
>
> *Jay Kesler, president emeritus of Taylor University*

In the old film *El Cid,* Charlton Heston, in the title role, was leading the Spanish army in a series of battles against the invading Moors. Just before the climactic confrontation, he was mortally wounded. His presence on the battlefield, however, was so important to the morale of his army that his officers fastened him in his saddle and propped him upright so he could lead his troops into the fray. Seeing their leader before them, the Spanish soldiers took heart and fought on to victory.

If El Cid had not been there, or if he had slumped in the saddle, his army might have lost heart and gone down to defeat.

Sometimes the best thing we can do is to simply "ride on" through the rough times. Our example may be just what others need to inspire them to keep going!

Don't Sit and Sulk; Face the Fearful

Crises in some form come to every leader. Those caused by evil intent can create anger and thirst for revenge. But responding like this limits a leader's ability to deal with the new realities.

In 2001, after the tragic events of 9/11, Billy Graham was called on to bring hope and meaning to his stunned fellow citizens. What could he say? He knew his message in the National Cathedral just three days after the devastation would be viewed by millions around the globe.

He communicated hope. "I've become an old man now," he said, "and the older I get, the more I cling to that hope that I started with many years ago." Billy spoke of Ambassador Andrew Young, who, after the tragic death of his wife, quoted from the old hymn "How Firm a Foundation":

"We all watched in horror as planes crashed into the steel and glass of the World Trade Center. Those majestic towers, built on solid foundations, were examples of the prosperity and creativity of America. When damaged, those buildings eventually plummeted to the ground, imploding upon themselves. Yet underneath the debris is a foundation that was not destroyed. Therein lies the truth of that old hymn that Andrew Young quoted: 'How *firm* a foundation.'

"Yes, our nation has been attacked. Buildings destroyed. Lives lost. But now we have a choice: whether to implode and disintegrate emotionally and spiritually as a people, and a nation, or, whether we choose to become stronger."

We may not be called on to speak to large audiences in crisis, but the small audiences we do have—maybe just one person—need to hear messages of hope. As Billy has said, "Men and women must have hope."

MOBILIZING MONEY

[Jesus said,] "I tell you, use your worldly resources
to benefit others and make friends. In this way, your
generosity stores up a reward for you in heaven."
LUKE 16:9 NLT

Said his younger brother Melvin, of Billy Graham,
"I've never seen a man in my life that cares as little
about money as Billy Frank does."

True? Yes, in that Billy has given away millions of
dollars of royalties and said no to countless offers to enrich
himself. Yet in many ways, he also cares a lot about money.
He recognizes that leaders can fall hard over it, that it can
seduce or blind or entrap. On the other hand, he knows
money has remarkable power to accomplish great ends.

He has always been determined not to waste money, but
to use it generously to further the vision of the ministry.

We talked to Mel about Billy's caution in spending
organizational money. Melvin described how Billy would
cut some projects "way down. He's just conscious of
God's money."…

We'd heard Billy was uncomfortable being seen in
fancy cars. Melvin told us stories of his refusing gift cars
and about his simple tastes. "Unless he was with somebody

like President Kennedy, he wouldn't even want to use a limousine. Today, over at the hotel, I said, 'Billy Frank, let me take you to the nice restaurant here.' He said, 'No, drop me over to McDonald's.' He got that from our momma and daddy."

Two things I ask of you, O LORD; …
Keep falsehood and lies far from me;
give me neither poverty nor riches,
but give me only my daily bread.
Otherwise, I may have too much and disown you
and say, 'Who is the LORD?'
Or I may become poor and steal,
and so dishonor the name of my God.

PROVERBS 30:7–9

While Billy has always been cautious and conservative when it comes to spending God's money, he has also been generous when he felt called to use it.

Sterling Huston, who serves as director of North American ministries for the BGEA, had his first experience with Billy Graham and money in 1956 before he joined the Graham team. "I was visiting Jack Wyrtzen's camp (Word of Life Camp, Schroon Lake, New York) on July 4. Billy preached, and Jack took up an offering for Billy and his ministry. After it was collected, however, Billy got up and said to the audience, 'With your permission, I want to give this to Jack for his dining room.' A fire had just damaged that part of Jack's main camp facility. Billy's magnanimity in giving the money to Jack left a deep impression on me. The generosity of spirit was typical of Billy. Because of his love and care for people, he's generous almost to a fault. And there was always transparent integrity about money."

In addition to being generous, Billy was always careful to avoid the appearance of improper use of the funds God had given his ministry.

Sterling said, "His strong concern was the ministry not be hurt by giving the wrong appearance about money. … When you look at 1987, for example, when some televangelists were in the headlines, it was very helpful to be able to say to the inquiring press that Billy didn't have a private plane, that he was driving an eleven-year-old car, that his home on the side of a mountain was a glorified log cabin, and that he gave away royalties to his books. That added greatly to his financial credibility."

Coming of age in the Great Depression showed him the consequences of inadequate funding. Tragic examples of leaders who used money selfishly made him viscerally opposed to feathering his own nest. Although he had many wealthy friends, he was acutely aware of the Bible's warnings about the love of money, and he was determined not to become personally entrapped. His own skills with money were unexceptional, but he saw money as a vital, God-given asset to be wisely employed. And, he knew that even with the best of intentions, financial sloppiness could spell disaster.

Billy's attitude was to listen and learn, always preparing for storms to come. That meant not only full financial disclosure, but maintaining integrity in many areas.

Dishonest money dwindles away,
but he who gathers money little by little makes it grow.
PROVERBS 13:11

*You will be made rich in every way so that
you can be generous on every occasion, and…
your generosity will result in thanksgiving to God.
This service that you perform is not only
supplying the needs of God's people but is also
overflowing in many expressions of thanks to God.*

2 CORINTHIANS 9:11–12

*Wisdom is a shelter
    as money is a shelter,
but the advantage of knowledge is this:
    that wisdom preserves the life of its possessor.*

ECCLESIASTES 7:12

*Keep your lives free from the love of money and be
    content with what you have, because God has said,
"Never will I leave you;
    never will I forsake you."
        So we say with confidence,
"The Lord is my helper; I will not be afraid.
    What can man do to me?"*

HEBREWS 13:5–6

MONEY

APPLYING THE PRINCIPLES

Jesus, it's said, spoke far more about money than about sex, violence, or heaven and hell. The subject is obviously important.

Leaders, especially, must exercise great wisdom about finances, for their decisions have such wide impact on others and on institutions, as well as on their own families.

ESTABLISH YOUR "MONEY DNA"

Billy Graham and his team aimed not to go first class but "in the middle." When David Schmidt first went to dinner with the Graham team, he was told, "Now, Dave, Billy taught us that we don't order the best thing on the menu, and we don't order the cheapest thing. We order in the middle." David says, "The rest of my days working with them, I just ordered in the middle. Middle hotel. Middle car. That was a formative financial value they instilled in me." Each of us must decide what works best for our team while still meeting high standards of integrity. Then, we develop a financial DNA that those we lead can follow.

REFINE YOUR PERSONAL ETHIC

Developing our personal financial ethics requires significant soul-searching and application of our deepest values. And it is a continuing process.

What do we need for ourselves? Should we all drive small economy cars? If we are among the fortunate, to what degree should we sacrifice? How can we genuinely help the poor? The answers are far from simple. Billy Graham has given away millions, but he has always wrestled with the fact that he has been given so much and the world's needs are so great.

In a world of consumerism...defining a financial ethic is a lifetime task—one that leaders should approach head-on with application of their best logic and commitments.

IF A PERSON GETS HIS ATTITUDE TOWARD MONEY STRAIGHT, IT WILL HELP STRAIGHTEN OUT ALMOST ANY OTHER AREA OF HIS LIFE.

Billy Graham

MATCH FINANCIAL HARNESSES THAT FIT

Once we have developed our personal convictions about money, we need to evaluate our personal skills. Here is where a team approach is critical. Generating funds, administrating them, strategizing their use—all are vital components. Strong, able players must be put into the best-fitting harnesses and given clear mandates.

Recognizing what we *don't* do well and must leave to others is as crucial as recognizing our strengths.

"Billy has always clearly seen he is a poor fund-raiser," one of his colleagues said about him. "He hates to ask people for money if he feels they are friends—hates to impose on their friendship. He doesn't want them to think he's interested in them only for their money."

At the same time, Billy grew up on a dairy farm, so he knew "he had to milk the cows every day or they'd go dry."

"He felt that you needed to keep asking for small amounts of money on a regular basis," said Fred Smith, one of Billy's board members.

Billy did what he did best, he built his constituency and made sure trustees and managers were in place to cover all the financial bases.

Scout People with Money Clues

When you're choosing people to help you further your vision, especially when it comes to financial aspects of that vision, give thoughtful observance…to where that person's heart really is when it comes to money, and what attitudes bleed through their words. The way a person feels about money can give you deep insight into his or her values.

Incorporate Billy's Essentials

Billy's approach to money is clear:
Be accountable to qualified others
Be transparent
Take money seriously
And above all, love God and people—not money

> THERE IS NOTHING WRONG WITH
> MEN POSSESSING RICHES. THE WRONG
> COMES WHEN RICHES POSSESS THEM.
>
> *Billy Graham*

Empowering Soul Mates

"There's a type of leadership that's ...
like a jazz bandleader who stands in
front of the ensemble tapping his foot
to set the rhythm. He points to the
piano player to take a few bars;
then he points to the saxophonist and
he does a riff. Likewise with the
drummer and bass player. They're all
playing the song, but at different
times, different people take
the lead doing different things,
which enhances but doesn't eclipse
the group's overall sound.
For fifty years the BGEA's mission
statement has been to support the
worldwide ministry of Billy Graham,"
Ross explains. "He definitely is the

LEADER, SETTING THE DIRECTION AND
THE PACE, BUT AT VARIOUS TIMES CERTAIN
MINISTRIES OR EMPHASES COME TO THE
FOREFRONT. BILLY BROUGHT GOOD PEOPLE
TO THE TEAM AND DEVISED A
BASIC STRATEGY AND OVERALL DIRECTION,
BUT HE GIVES THEM ROOM TO DO WHAT
THEY HAVE TO DO FOR THEIR
PARTICULAR ASPECT OF THE MINISTRY."

*A. Larry Ross, Billy's longtime media and
public relations consultant*

Billy's relationship with Sherwood "Woody" Wirt shows Billy's ability to find soul mates and then give them the room they need to grow and thrive using their own unique talents.

Sherwood Wirt was the first editor of Billy's *Decision* magazine, and was indeed a soul mate to Billy. A pastor, an Edinburgh PhD, a journalist, and a free spirit, Sherwood Wirt brought to the magazine far more than the usual competence of a house-organ editor. In *Decision* magazine he published Billy's sermons and ministry news, but he also included articles such as a thoughtful yet accessible series on Russian author Fyodor Dostoyevsky, complete with compelling original art. He knew Billy's vision was to take the magazine to a higher level, and he stretched to do so.

In his book, simply titled *Billy*, Sherwood gives insight into how Graham connected with respected teammates, how he cultivated them, worked beside them, inspired, and entrusted them.

First of all, Billy immersed "Woody" in the vision, the dream, and the action of the ministry. A few months after Billy's invitation over the phone to Sherwood to be the editor of *Decision*, the evangelist was experiencing the largest crowds of his career in Australia, and he brought his new editor right into the middle of it.

Billy prayed with Sherwood. The effect on Woody of those few minutes on their knees had its own power: "I rose, feeling greatly refreshed. A final word, a handshake, and I was out the door and on my way to the airport and across the Pacific, bursting with anticipation of what the Lord was about to do."

Billy gave Woody detailed instructions. He wrote a lengthy, well-constructed letter with many specific ideas as they began the process of shaping the magazine. But Billy also ended the letter with both a challenge and warmth. "This is quite a big order; however, I believe it can be done and will meet a real need. I believe the Lord has led you to this important ministry and am thankful for your willingness to obey His voice in this matter."

Billy kept up the drumbeat of communication, even after the magazine was up and running. He helped Woody realize the high stakes involved and kept him focused on the quality expected. He also cheered him on. After the first issue came out, Billy wrote, "Dear Woody: Just a note to say I have read through your manuscript for the first issue of *Decision*. I think it is terrific!"

Billy also supported and defended Sherwood. On one occasion, Woody had interviewed a prominent person, then sent the edited version to the interviewee— who strongly objected to a deletion! He said the interview must run in its entirety or not at all. Unfortunately, Woody faced an immediate deadline and published the edited interview.

When that issue of *Decision* came out, the man was furious. He immediately called Billy to object. In responding to the irate man, Billy didn't put Woody in a bad light. He told the man that he'd always seen his editor act with integrity, then apologized for the incident. In a later discussion with Woody, he reassured him, but he also counseled, "Next time, Woody, don't get caught so close to the deadline. Protect yourself."

Billy sought the balance of praise blended with expectations for learning and growth. He guided and encouraged his team. He praised them highly, always wanting to ensure that they understood how much he valued them. Billy's voice communicated optimism, love, and a strong sense of purpose.

Some have called Billy's example the "Graham DNA." This DNA permeated Billy's organization, filling its leaders with the same values and strengths Billy himself showed.

Billy trusted those around him, which in turn helped his team to find others to trust who would be assets to the team.

Billy had a drive toward excellence, which required thoroughness and hard work. This caused his team to strive for the highest standards as well.

Most of all, because of Billy's grace-filled way of dealing with others, his team tried to model grace in all they did as well.

Billy's DNA caused a wonderful ripple effect throughout his team causing them to say along with him: "I'm called to do this, no matter what the challenges. Join me!"

EMPOWERING

APPLYING THE PRINCIPLES

At the core of leadership is guiding and empowering those we lead. When we do so with skill, love, and grace, the effects radiate far beyond those we personally touch.

UNLEASH AND MULTIPLY

The leader with a large vision knows the means of accomplishment is to select those with great capacities who can slash their own trail through the thickets and get the job done. But it's far more than mere selection and assignment. Delegation means providing clear, simple "lines" and freedom, but also generating strong loyalties and a sense that each person's contribution is highly valued.

WHEN BILLY ASKS YOU TO DO SOMETHING,
YOU KIND OF WANT TO FIND A WAY TO DO IT.
YOU DON'T WANT TO LET HIM DOWN.

Carl Henry, first editor of Christianity Today

Don't Dominate—Lead!

On first reading the statement, one might object that countless leaders of great accomplishment have powerfully dominated others. Yet if a leader today is to unleash the full potential of others, domination will severely limit the soaring of the followers' spirits and effectiveness. Billy Graham never dominated, but in thousands of connections he inspired and led.

Light Fires, Communicate Trust

Know how to put fire into your subordinates.

Jesuit philosopher Baltasar Graciàn

Putting fire into others starts with integrity and a significant cause. Yet the flames need to be fanned regularly, and a primary way to do that is through praise.

If anything, Billy would praise people a bit more than they might deserve. He would claim more of the fault for problems as his own. But this was not manipulation. His colleagues knew he really felt that way about their contributions, as well as their importance as persons, and that he saw his own role in a humble light.

Set the Pace!

The leader raises the bar and knows that he or she must be first to meet its demands. The leader must set the pace and communicate enthusiasm for running the race. A commitment to championship goals in any endeavor sets all eyes on the significant challenge.

Many leaders try to do all the major lifting themselves, and then bask in the limelight. It's a constant temptation.

When we talked with David Schmidt, media consultant, about Billy's experiences, he said, "I wish I could help your readers understand what it's like to have the state and local police pull up in a motorcade and escort you to the lower bowels of a stadium through a back door. There's so much that says, 'You, you, you. You're a rock star! You're it!' Billy goes down the line shaking hands, meeting dignitaries, and everything is saying, 'You're important.' But Billy kept saying, 'No, it's not for my glory. God won't share his glory, so I need to get down so he can get up.' When you have a leader at the top who says, 'This is not about me,' that's big!"

Whatever was to my profit I now consider loss
for the sake of Christ. What is more,
I consider everything a loss compared to the surpassing
greatness of knowing Christ Jesus my Lord,
for whose sake I have lost all things. I consider them
rubbish, that I may gain Christ.

PHILIPPIANS 3:7–8

Expanding the
Growing Edge

Leaders often find themselves not only caught between forces but struggling to come to their own conclusions. In today's acceleration of change and emergence of global ideas and methods, sharp divisions put leaders in precarious positions.

For Billy, in the 1950s, the gathering storm of racial issues forced him to search deeply the Scriptures and his own soul. From our perspective a half century later, we may wonder why he would have any question whatsoever about "the right thing to do." But immersed in the churning currents of beliefs in America at that time, he truly was caught in a dilemma.

At first Graham tried to carve a middle ground that opposed both forced integration as well as forced segregation. He relied on the example of Billy Sunday, who had followed local custom by preaching to integrated audiences in the North and to mostly segregated audiences in the South. So, in many of his earliest meetings, Graham followed suit.

But the dramatic times left little maneuvering room for moderates. Reporters demanded to know why he could not speak to integrated audiences in South Carolina and Georgia just as he did in California and

Massachusetts. They asked why he never addressed racism in the South.

Billy chose to make his stand in the heart of the segregated South. He initially agreed to segregate the audience during his 1952 campaign in Jackson, Mississippi, but rejected Governor Hugh White's suggestion to conduct separate meetings for blacks. Meanwhile Billy prepared to make a much bolder statement. Holding segregated events had always struck him as wrong, but he'd never chosen to take decisive action—until now. Walking toward the ropes that separated blacks and whites, Billy tore them down.

Mystified and uncomfortable ushers tried to put the ropes back up. Billy personally stopped them.

This symbolically powerful gesture marked a major ministry watershed. He never again led a segregated campaign.

It may be that had it not been for a black man, we would never have heard of Billy Graham. On the Charlotte dairy farm, as he was growing up, his family employed an African-American foreman and treated him as a valued member of the family. In 1933, when evangelistic meetings were being held in town, young Billy didn't want to go. He had no interest in it—but as a new driver, he did have a strong interest in driving the foreman's truck.

"Tell you what. I'll let you drive my truck if you'll go to the crusade with me," the older man offered.

Billy accepted the deal, and that led to his conversion. The concerned foreman, who was like family, represented one of the roots of Billy's sensitivity on racial issues.

Later, Billy invited Dr. Martin Luther King to give a prayer at his New Your City evangelistic meetings, a symbolic move that further solidified his commitment to the movement toward racial equality. "A great social revolution is going on in the United States today," Billy said as he introduced King. "Dr. King is one of its leaders, and we appreciate his taking time out of his busy schedule to come and share this service with us tonight."

Billy's relationship with King affords a telling glimpse into Billy's strategy. He sympathized with King's motives and admired his peaceful tactics, but he also recognized that much of his own core constituency was not ready for civil disobedience. Billy broke custom and tradition where necessary, but he would not break the law. This cautious approach doesn't impress many modern observers, who eagerly point out how much more Billy could have done to aid King's cause. At the time, however, Billy bolstered King's agenda among a constituency not yet reached by civil rights activists. Billy knew his followers and their limitations, identified their growing edge, and helped shape their perspectives on race relations.

In your hearts set apart Christ as Lord.
Always be prepared to give an answer to everyone who
asks you to give the reason for the hope that you have.
But do this with gentleness and respect.

1 PETER 3:15

NOTHING IS SO STRONG AS GENTLENESS,
NOTHING SO GENTLE AS REAL STRENGTH.

Francis de Sales

The Lord's servants must not quarrel
but must be kind to everyone. They must be able
to teach effectively and be patient with difficult people.
They should gently teach those who oppose the truth.
Perhaps God will change those people's hearts,
and they will believe the truth.

2 TIMOTHY 2:24–25 NLT

> LET YOUR DEALING WITH THOSE YOU BEGIN
> WITH BE SO GENTLE, CONVINCING, AND
> WINNING, THAT THE REPORT OF IT MAY BE AN
> ENCOURAGEMENT TO OTHERS TO COME.
>
> *Richard Baxter*

THE GROWING EDGE

APPLYING THE PRINCIPLES

It's easy to lament and critique leaders; but it's another thing entirely to skillfully, and with integrity, lead without losing one's followers or convictions. Billy had to drive stakes in the ground that would maintain his integrity yet not jeopardize his primary mission when it came to dealing with race issues. How can we effectively lead in this area of helping others gently grow without pushing them too far?

ESTABLISH CONVICTIONS

Billy would listen carefully to a multitude of counselors before he formed his own convictions on racial justice. A conviction is but a shallow idea if it is simply reflective of how one was raised or as a response to persuasive voices. Issues are complex, and forming conviction takes depth of analysis and careful probing of one's soul.

Once established, convictions must be nurtured by fresh evaluations as new circumstances and information arise.

KNOW THE EDGE

If we don't have a good grasp of people's intensities and beliefs on an issue, we face two limitations. First, we won't know how to articulate our convictions in ways that communicate effectively to those who waver or disagree. Second, we will be blindsided by unexpected reactions. Leadership, by its nature, requires strong convictions but also the skills to effectively communicate those convictions and to back off emphases that will deflect from the main focus of your mission.

BE PATIENT LIKE LINCOLN AND ROOSEVELT

Lincoln chose to move slowly when he decided to issue the Emancipation Proclamation, carefully preparing the nation for this monumental change.

Roosevelt foresaw as early as 1937 that the United States would very likely be drawn into war with Europe. He slowly awakened the public mind to the dangers outside and prepared it for eventual sacrifice.

It often takes time and patience to communicate tough and controversial necessities, yet both are needed to generate enthusiastic support.

USE NATURAL FORCES

Often it's not arguments but positive natural dynamics that break down barriers and bring understanding to people alienated from each other. Billy brought white and black Americans together at his 1976 meetings in Jackson, Mississippi. As a result many of them began praying together, singing in the choir together, and studying the Bible together. They began to really know each other as real people. Billy's nurturing of the growing edge of people's racial understandings had a powerful effect.

RESPECT THE MLKs

You never know when someone who sees things quite differently will go on to make a huge impact—and will have been right about many things. Martin Luther King Jr. shared Graham's roots in the gospel but had been trained in a liberal seminary and had a different agenda. Billy could have simply avoided him and dodged a lot of criticism from many in his constituency. At the same time, he had developed convictions in tune with King's, and he sought common ground.

Martin Luther King Jr. once told Billy, "I believe your crusades are doing more to break down racial barriers and to bring the races together than what I'm doing. Your work is helping me."

In a world increasingly polarized and bitter, Billy Graham has shown how one can maintain integrity, continue to grow personally, and to carefully communicate the fruit of that growth to others' growing edge.

At times we may be tempted to use the pit-bull tactics so prevalent around us. But Billy shows how respect for those he leads and respect for those with whom he disagrees can result in growth and great progress in fulfilling a mission.

We ought always to thank God for you …
because your faith is growing more and more, and the
love every one of you has for each other is increasing.
2 Thessalonians 1:3

PART FOUR

GROWING *Through*
FIRE & ICE

Over the years, any leader will
come up against events that either
dramatically deepen the person or
generate bitterness of soul.

*Billy allowed the difficult times in
his ministry to teach him about:
summoning courage,
learning from failure,
experiencing trauma and
betrayal without growing bitter,
and redeeming the ego.*

*He developed a tough hide and a
tender heart.*

SUMMONING COURAGE

Leaders are out in full view; each one becomes a target, and each must anticipate being shot at. They must sense the challenge and rise above the natural reactions to lash out or shrink back, to summon courage and tenacity to lead when the stakes are high and the results could be failure or humiliation.

At times on many initiatives, Billy diligently and with great thoroughness sought wisdom and counsel, then devoted full energies to implementing a plan of action—only to see his efforts assaulted. Perhaps no greater example of that was his experience on his return from his historic trip to Russia in 1982.

His vision for ministry in the Soviet Union had begun long before. In 1959, though unable to get permission to hold meetings there, he visited the Soviet Union as a tourist. Sitting with friend and ministry partner Grady Wilson, Billy gazed across the vast expanse of an empty Lenin Stadium in Moscow. The great coliseum, site of Soviet athletic triumphs and numerous Communist Party celebrations, felt strangely impotent without the throngs of Russian spectators. He envisioned standing before those masses, preaching the good news of Christ in a country where God had been outlawed.

Communist officials had barred him from speaking publicly, so instead Billy simply bowed his head and prayed that God would one day bring him back to the Soviet capital and allow him to share the gospel.

Billy continued this prayer for many years, until, eventually, after long and complex negotiations, Communist authorities gave a green light, with some conditions.

Billy would not be permitted to preach in any of Russia's great stadiums, as he had prayed in 1959, but he would be able to speak in both Baptist and Orthodox churches. There was just one catch: he would also be expected to participate in a gathering called "The World Conference of Religious Workers for Saving the Sacred Gift of Life from Nuclear Catastrophe." That was a problem. Despite the noble-sounding purpose and religious sponsorship, such meetings were infamous for being Communist-manipulated, anti-American propaganda events.

Billy agonized over the decision. When Billy asked their advice, Allan Emery and George Bennett counseled him not to go, believing the risk to his reputation was too great if the Soviets used him for political gain.

In contrast, Dr. Alexander Haraszti, a Hungarian Baptist, adamantly said he should go, arguing that "the Lord has opened the door, and we must enter the door. …You must not jeopardize the ten years to come. This is the beginning.…"

But Billy's friend, Vice President George H. W. Bush, called him to tell him the U.S. ambassador to the Soviet Union did not want him to go. Billy was torn by compelling arguments on both sides.

Finally, he decided to accept the invitations, and his ministry in Russia turned out to be remarkable. Baptists and Pentecostals and Orthodox all welcomed him. He presented the gospel clearly and without restriction in his preaching and in private conversations.

Throughout the trip, though, Billy's comments, meant to be gracious and evenhanded, were interpreted as naive. Back home in the U.S., the media was sharply critical.

The media accused him of making a fool of himself, of abandoning persecuted Russian Christians, and of pandering to the Communist officials. Even one of his allies, Edmund Robb, surprised him during a televised interview by saying, "I am convinced you've made a serious mistake in your visit to the Soviet Union, and if some of the things you've been quoted as saying are true, they've certainly compromised you with a great deal of the evangelical community."

When leaders take risks and find themselves not only in the bull's-eye but deep in the pits, it takes courage to go out and continue to face the assaults. But Billy did. He weathered the emotional hits and stayed the course. Ultimately, Billy was vindicated for his historic 1982 trip, but he couldn't know that at the time. He had to simply keep soldiering on and accept the harsh realities of the assaults. For Billy, the only critic who really counted was God.

When they hurled their insults at [Christ], he did not retaliate; when he suffered, he made no threats. Instead, he entrusted himself to him who judges justly.

1 PETER 2:23

In 1992, Billy stood again in Moscow's Olympic Stadium, where he had prayed as a tourist in 1959. Only now, the stadium was not empty. This time Billy shared the message of God's love with 50,000 people crammed in a stadium built for 38,000. Between 20,000 and 30,000 additional people stood outside watching the crusade on projection screens.

COURAGE

APPLYING THE PRINCIPLES

Leadership and fear—the two seem to be opposites.
A leader steps out "fearlessly." Yet fear and leadership are
intertwined—not just in the "great moments" of high
danger. We daily must make decisions and take risks that
call for courage.

EMBRACE COURAGE—IN THE ORDINARY, AND IN CHAOS

If we have courage, it means we are overcoming fear, and
leaders—in addition to natural human fears—have the
added weight of communicating unpleasant realities or
being misunderstood. The challenges keep growing, and
the acceleration of change can turn our decisions and
plans into disaster. But courage means we count the cost,
make our best decisions, and lead on.

RECOGNIZE FEAR AS A CATALYST FOR COURAGE

Fear is an ally. Fear is a catalyst. Fear helps equip us to lead.
In all the ordinary demands of leadership, fear emerges,
and we can either make it a catalyst for courage or a
culprit leading to cowardice.

I HAVE ENJOYED MYSELF MOST WHEN
I HAVE BEEN AT MY BEST, AND I HAVE BEEN
MOST OFTEN AT MY BEST WHEN I'VE
BEEN BADLY SCARED. I FOUND THAT FEAR
HAS AROUSED IN ME UNSUSPECTED POWERS.

I. A. R. Wylie, writer

Brace Yourself—And Take Action

The key, whether it's facing a life-threatening event or a speaking engagement, is to confront the fear we feel. Life is full of fearsome things, and the requirements of leadership increase our risk. Courage comes when we swallow our fears, sensing within how much our response changes everything—even when the worst happens.

It is God who arms me with strength
and makes my way perfect.
He makes my feet like the feet of a deer;
he enables me to stand on the heights.
He trains my hands for battle;
my arms can bend a bow of bronze.
You give me your shield of victory,
and your right hand sustains me;
you stoop down to make me great.
PSALM 18:32–35

LOOK FEAR IN THE FACE...
YOU GAIN STRENGTH, COURAGE, AND
CONFIDENCE...YOU MUST DO THE THING
YOU THINK YOU CANNOT DO.

Eleanor Roosevelt

Build "Dikes of Courage"

The night before he was murdered in Memphis, Martin Luther King, Jr. talked about the threats from "some of our sick white brothers." Then he said, "Well, I don't know what will happen now. We've got some difficult days ahead. But it doesn't matter with me now. Because I've been to the mountaintop. And I don't mind. Like anybody, I would like to live a long life. Longevity has its place. But I'm not concerned about that now. I just want to do God's will. And He's allowed me to go up to the mountain. And I've looked over. And I've seen the promised land. I may not get there with you. But I want you to know tonight, that we, as a people, will get to the promised land. And I'm happy, tonight. I'm not worried about anything. I'm not fearing any man. Mine eyes have seen the glory of the coming of the Lord."

The next day he was shot.

Said King, "We must constantly build dikes of courage to hold back the flood of fear."

King led with enormous courage, though he surely felt "the flood of fear." We may not face challenges as dangerous or tragic, but we can apply his drumbeat of affirmations to a wide range of our own leadership challenges.

Fear the Right Things

The Bible says God is holy and hates the evil that visits horrors on his people and his creation. So throughout the Bible we read a drumbeat of commands to "Fear God." And it's a remarkable paradox of fear and joy. In the Psalms we read:

Happy are those who fear the Lord.
Praise the LORD, all you who fear him!
Serve the LORD with reverent fear and rejoice.

A strange mixture—rejoicing in fear. Yet it's a matter of rightly placed fear. In this case, it's the ultimate fear that the Scriptures say gives ultimate joy.

May those who fear [the LORD] rejoice.
PSALM 119:74

LEARNING FROM FAILURE

Being a leader means more opportunities for doing good. But it also means that the costs are higher for failure. Failures produce magnified consequences when we are in positions of leadership because they affect not just ourselves but also our followers and our cause.

Failure is the inevitable companion of a large vision. No one can take on a significant and difficult challenge without stumbling a few times. The important thing is how we respond. The goal is not a fail-safe record but a pattern of increasing effectiveness.

Meeting President Truman

One of Billy's early failures, an embarrassing gaffe following a meeting with President Truman, showed him to be one who recognized and corrected his mistakes with speed and grace. This humiliating moment, interestingly, is the incident Billy uses to begin his autobiography, *Just As I Am.* This failure prepared him for a lifetime of significant encounters with world leaders.

Upon emerging from the White House, the press corps asked: "What did you tell the president, and what did he say?" Billy, not knowing he was violating diplomatic protocol, told them everything he could remember.

"It began to dawn on me a few days later how we had abused the privilege of seeing the president," said Billy. "The president was offended that I had quoted him without authorization."

Billy tried to make amends. But Truman had informed his aides that "when, as, and if a request comes for Billy Graham to be received at the White House, the president requests that it be turned down."

Billy eventually became a confidant of popes and presidents and prime ministers because he had learned to keep conversations in confidence.

My flesh and my heart may fail,
but God is the strength of my heart
and my portion forever.
Psalm 73:26

IT IS NOBLER TO TRY SOMETHING
AND FAIL THAN TO TRY NOTHING AND
SUCCEED. THE RESULT MAY BE THE SAME,
BUT YOU WON'T BE. WE ALWAYS GROW MORE
THROUGH DEFEATS THAN VICTORIES.

Author Unknown

If the LORD delights in a man's way,
*   he makes his steps firm;*
though he stumble, he will not fall,
*   for the LORD upholds him with his hand.*

PSALM 37:23–24

THERE IS THE GREATEST PRACTICAL BENEFIT IN MAKING A FEW FAILURES EARLY IN LIFE.

Thomas Huxley

APPLYING THE PRINCIPLES

Failures can lead eventually to great accomplishment, but of course they can also stop a leader cold and destroy his or her effectiveness. Much of it depends on whether or not we have, at the critical times, the…wisdom to embrace these central principles.

USE FAILURE AS AN ASSET

What do Henry Ford, Winston Churchill, and Abraham Lincoln have in common? They all faced failure. As *Peter Pan* author J. M. Barrie said, "We are all failures—at least, all the best of us are." Failure is painful when it happens, but it can become one of our greatest assets if we allow it to help us grow.

Train Yourself for Failure

Make peace with the fact that you will fail sometimes. Mistakes are not irreversible. Keep everything in perspective. Observe any high achiever, and you'll discover a person who doesn't see a mistake as the enemy.

> THE FELLOW WHO NEVER MAKES A MISTAKE
> TAKES HIS ORDERS FROM THE ONE WHO DOES.
>
> *Herbert V. Procknow*

Take Risks

Giving in to our fears of taking risks stunts our capacity for growth. Taking risks day after day, year after year, equals some failures. It's simple math. Yet risk is a necessity for leadership and success.

Grab the Bull's Tail

Each must lead with lots of self-understanding, wise counsel, and judicious analysis. But for all of us, times come when we have to make that decision: grab the bull by the tail or let it go by.

> A PERSON WHO HAS HAD A BULL BY THE TAIL
> ONCE HAS LEARNED SIXTY OR SEVENTY TIMES
> AS MUCH AS THE PERSON WHO HASN'T.
>
> *Mark Twain*

Turn Even Unthinkable Failure into Gold

Failures come in many ways, some our fault, others not. Taking risks opens us to consequences, and as we lead and take those risks, it doesn't hurt to ask, "What if the very worst happens to me?" Obviously, the answer starts with how the decision to take action was made, and the hopefully good process and good counsel that led to it. But beyond that, in the "furnace of affliction," the reality is that out of the worst can come remarkable things.

> MOUNTAINTOPS ARE FOR VIEWS
> AND INSPIRATION,
> BUT FRUIT IS GROWN IN THE VALLEYS.
>
> *Billy Graham*

Experiencing Trauma and Betrayal

What is the most painful experience you can have as a leader? Many would say being betrayed by someone you fully trusted, someone with whom you'd let down your guard and become fully vulnerable.

In many ways, leadership is relationships, and if we are effective leaders, generally we need to build close ones. We are wary at first of trusting anyone too much. We recognize our judgments about whom we can trust must be accurate, or we can suffer deeply.

Yet sometimes even the most astute leaders get blindsided by someone good at projecting sincerity and friendship, yet with a different agenda. How you respond when it happens can make the difference between continuing a vigorous leadership or falling as a casualty.

What was the most painful thing Billy Graham experienced in his long years as a leader? What shook him to his core? According to his wife, Ruth, it was his feeling of being betrayed by Richard Nixon when the Watergate transcripts were made public. Ruth said it was the hardest thing her husband had ever gone through.

Billy built his friendship with Nixon when he was vice president under Dwight Eisenhower. When Nixon failed to defeat Kennedy in his own bid to become president in 1960, and two years later lost the election for governor of California, he was devastated. Once excruciatingly close to the Oval Office, Nixon sank into depression. It seemed only a few still believed in Nixon—but one who did was his longtime friend, Billy Graham. Billy's respect for Nixon was genuine and deep. He admired his intellectual capabilities and government expertise.

In 1967, Nixon called Billy for advice. The political tide had once again turned. Down and out for five years, Nixon had reclaimed much of his earlier luster. Now he wanted Billy's opinion on making another run for the White House, so he invited Billy to join him in Florida. During two days in Key Biscayne, Nixon and Billy discussed Scripture and prayed, as they frequently did when together.

Later, Nixon said that Billy, more than any other individual, influenced his decision to run.

Years later, when Nixon fell, Billy's embarrassment stung because the president had betrayed him publicly as a visible ally and privately as a close friend. The association with Nixon tarnished Billy's ministry and legacy, and Billy wondered how he could have been so wrong about him.

And for Richard Nixon, Billy had reached out far "beyond the call of duty." Despite the pain of betrayal, despite the embarrassment, despite the questions of "How?" and "Why?"—Billy never gave up on him.

Even after Nixon left the White House in disgrace, Billy refused to pile on. "I shall always consider him a personal friend," he told reporters. "His personal suffering must be almost unbearable. He deserves the prayers even of those who feel betrayed and let down."

Billy's love for the man who betrayed his trust

remained strong. As with many other traumas he had experienced in leading, he did not let natural reactions of self-pity or anger control his responses. Billy, in living through the nightmare had, because of the depth of his faith and commitments, once again become a stronger leader, tempered by the fires.

BETRAYAL

APPLYING THE PRINCIPLES

Resilient leaders recognize early that life can be difficult, and they do what they can to endure, to deepen and grow, and to keep leading. So what can we do to prepare?

TRAIN FOR THE NEXT EMOTIONAL HIT

We seldom think of calamities as opportunities for growth, especially when they send us reeling. But of course, they always are. In hindsight, we sometimes see that out of the worst came far deeper understanding of ourselves and of the human condition—a crucial component of effective leadership.

TOUGH INDIVIDUALS ARE CONSISTENTLY
ABLE TO PERCEIVE STRESSFUL SITUATIONS AS
OPPORTUNITIES FOR GROWTH.

James E. Loehr, author of
Toughness Training for Life

BITTER MEDICINE IN YOUR MOUTH?
CHECK THE DIRECTIONS

Leaders have many occasions to feel bitter. We can let it fester or we can deal with it. Turn to the Bible's advice: "See to it that no one misses the grace of God and that no bitter root grows up to cause trouble and defile many" (Hebrews 12:15). A leader who is bitter certainly will cause trouble, for himself or herself and for many others.

Though my father and mother forsake me,
    the LORD will receive me.
                    PSALM 27:10

The LORD loves the just
    and will not forsake his faithful ones.
They will be protected forever.
                    PSALM 37:28

> GOD IS NOT A DECEIVER, THAT HE SHOULD
> OFFER TO SUPPORT US, AND THEN, WHEN WE
> LEAN UPON HIM, SHOULD SLIP AWAY FROM US.
>
> *Augustine of Hippo*

> *At my first defense, no one came to my support,*
> *but everyone deserted me. May it not be held against*
> *them. But the Lord stood at my side and*
> *gave me strength, so that through me the message*
> *might be fully proclaimed.*
>
> 2 TIMOTHY 4:16–17

METAMORPHOSIZE!

Sometimes traumas make us desperate. Sometimes they may literally bring us to the edge of emotional or physical death. Not everyone calling out to God in such times experiences a metamorphosis. Such experiences, however, do show the power of turning from overwhelming troubles to the spiritual power that can lead to personal transformation.

Blessed is the man who perseveres under trial,
because when he has stood the test,
he will receive the crown of life that
God has promised to those who love him.

JAMES 1:12

OUT OF THE DEPTHS, COMMUNICATE HOPE

Leaders, of course, must endure not only their own
tragedies but those of others as well. When storms strike
individuals or organizations, a leader who responds with
genuine concern and calm establishes his or her leadership.
We experience our own pain but simultaneously identify
with what others feel and think, reaching out to them.

BANDAGE YOUR WOUNDS, AND DRIVE!

We all experience "emotional hits," and we can't deny
them. Even though we may find ourselves hurting
badly—very badly—we may still have to lead others.

In the movie *Black Hawk Down* a vehicle filled with
wounded American soldiers lurches to a stop in the
middle of a street where Somali bullets are flying in every
direction. The officer in charge tells a soldier to get in
and start driving. "I can't," the soldier says, "I'm shot."

Sometimes, as leaders, bullets not only fly but hit us right in the gut, disabling us.

But in *Black Hawk Down*, the officer uses this immortal line after the soldier says he's shot: "We're all shot. Get in and drive!"

The human condition. We're all wounded, but we have to keep going anyway. Sometimes these are words to live by: "We're all shot. Get in and drive."

COMFORT AND PROSPERITY
HAVE NEVER ENRICHED THE WORLD
AS MUCH AS ADVERSITY HAS.

Billy Graham

REDEEMING THE EGO

Billy commands respect from presidents, from Ike, Johnson—all of them!" said Bill Mead, Graham's first executive committee chair. Fred Smith, another longtime colleague of Billy's, added, "Billy was humble but not intimidated."

How could someone be humble and handle the ego while becoming such close friends with presidents?

"The ego must be redeemed," Fred replied.

Billy's ability to command respect at the highest levels and to turn hostile reporters into advocates would naturally inflate anyone's ego. Yet, when you speak to Billy's colleagues and friends, his humility is a constant theme.

You have to have a strong ego to lead, but something must happen to it—you must allow God to redeem it.

What does it really mean to "redeem your ego"? Many instances in Billy's life show how he deliberately gave his ego over to the Lord.

Graeme Keith, treasurer of Billy's organization, tells this story:

"I was on an elevator with Billy when another man in the elevator recognized him. He said, 'You're Billy Graham, aren't you?'

'Yes,' Billy said.

'Well,' he said, 'you are truly a great man.'

"Billy immediately responded, 'No, I'm not a great man. I just have a great message.'"

Graeme went on to tell of the time when he was with Billy in a group setting. A leader in the organization was describing in detail Billy's accomplishments. "He told everyone about all the many things he had done," Graeme said. "But then Billy interrupted him. He said, 'No, that's not right. I didn't do these things. The Lord did.'"

From those who have known him best emerges the picture of Billy's unfeigned belief that he was simply God's ambassador, carrying a message of love to the world. His oft-repeated remark that "my lips would turn to clay if God took his hand from me" gave him a sense that he was, to use Mother Teresa's description of herself, "God's pencil."

We see here Billy's self-perception of being a simple workman with a huge mandate, like an ambassador in wartime carrying gold bullion to people desperately needing it. He's the conveyer of the most important goods in the world, and he believes all is lost or won depending on how he carries the message and how he responds to God's initiatives.

> MOST OF ALL, IF ANYTHING HAS BEEN ACCOMPLISHED THROUGH MY LIFE, IT HAS BEEN SOLELY GOD'S DOING, NOT MINE, AND HE — NOT I — MUST GET THE CREDIT.
>
> *Billy Graham*

> [Jesus said,] *"Remain in me, and I will remain in you. No branch can bear fruit by itself; it must remain in the vine. Neither can you bear fruit unless you remain in me. I am the vine; you are the branches. If a man remains in me and I in him, he will bear much fruit; apart from me you can do nothing. If anyone does not remain in me, he is like a branch that is thrown away and withers; such branches are picked up, thrown into the fire and burned. If you remain in me and my words remain in you, ask whatever you wish, and it will be given you."*
>
> JOHN 15:4–7

It seems like a difficult task—balancing a humble attitude with the bold spirit of a leader. "Blessed are the meek," said Jesus. When we hear this, we are likely to think of a mouse—definitely not someone strong and spirited. And yet, to truly understand the Bible's use of the word "meek," we might look to the image used by poet and Franciscan nun, Mary Karr.

She says we should picture a great stallion at full gallop. At his master's voice, he "seizes up to a stunned but instant halt." Karr then describes the stallion holding its "great power" in check, listening for the next order.

True meekness is power under God's control.

LEADERSHIP LESSONS:

EGO

APPLYING THE PRINCIPLES

The word *ego* has at least two definitions:

A regarding of one's self with undue favor.

A sense of one's own dignity or worth.

Redeeming the ego can be described as how effectively our own ego is marked by the second definition rather than the first.

What are the ways that leaders can harness the power of ego so that it doesn't hinder but instead serves the cause?

HUMILITY IS NOT DENYING THE POWER YOU HAVE. IT IS REALIZING THAT THE POWER COMES THROUGH YOU, NOT FROM YOU.

Fred Smith

BE AWARE OF MYSTERIOUS FORCES

Great forces are at work that are beyond our comprehension, and that awareness has an enormous impact on the ego.

ONE MUST DO ONE'S DUTY TO THE BEST OF ONE'S ABILITY, WHATEVER THE COST, WHATEVER THE CIRCUMSTANCES, AND TRUST THAT PROVIDENCE WILL TURN EVERYTHING, EVEN APPARENT DISASTER, TO SOME USEFUL PURPOSE, HOWEVER DIMLY PERCEIVED, IF IT CAN BE PERCEIVED AT ALL.

General Robert E. Lee

In Humiliation, Lead On

In the time of humiliation, leadership is needed all the more, and one's perspective will determine whether you fold or step up to a very different sort of challenge. A leader is called to view the situation from a higher plane, to see beyond the immediate situation to the long-term consequences.

Humiliation, while always painful, is a deepening and purifying process—Jesus himself is our primary model of suffering the ultimate humiliation with extreme grace.

Your attitude should be the same as that of Christ Jesus:
Who, being in very nature God,
did not consider equality with God something to
be grasped,
but made himself nothing,
taking the very nature of a servant,
being made in human likeness.
And being found in appearance as a man,
he humbled himself
and became obedient to death—
even death on a cross!
PHILIPPIANS 2:5–8

Think Large; It's Not Egocentric

Missionary statesman Frank Laubach lived with zest and productivity, traveling the globe and writing more than fifty books. He received many honors, and when presented with a Man of the Year Award said, "The Lord will not wish to count my trophies, but my scars."

He had his world-class accomplishments and his ego in perspective.

And yet, with that perspective—that earthly accomplishment meant little—he prayed, "God, what have you to put into my mind now if only I can be large enough?" He thought a waiting, eager attitude would "give God the chance He needs," and apparently it did. From that time, until he died at age eighty-five, Laubach accomplished "large" things far beyond his dreams.

Dreaming big dreams pleases God when you're dreaming for him.

With God all things are possible.
Matthew 19:26

Avoid "Grievous Peril"

Thomas à Kempis wrote, "Those who stand highest in the esteem of men are most exposed to grievous peril." Billy was thoroughly aware of that danger: "I feel that people have put me on too high a pedestal. We do the same with other leaders. I know, however, that I am not as good as some people think I am. I have seen men in the depths of wickedness and I have thought to myself, 'There I go except by the grace of God.'"

When I consider your heavens,
   the work of your fingers,
the moon and the stars,
   which you have set in place,
what is man that you are mindful of him,
   the son of man that you care for him?
You made him a little lower than the heavenly beings
   and crowned him with glory and honor.
You made him ruler over the works of your hands;
   you put everything under his feet. ...
O LORD, our Lord,
   how majestic is your name in all the earth!
                    PSALM 8:3–6, 9

MULTIPLYING
MOMENTUM

Billy's leadership built momentum all the way through his more than sixty years of ministry. What maintained and kept that momentum going?

Billy dreamed of new initiatives and actually did them. He also built bridges to leaders of constituencies in many ways the opposite to his own.

Billy mentored many strong leaders worldwide, and he kept planting seeds that bore diversified fruit.

BIRTHING DREAMS

The entrepreneurial leader is always dreaming of what might be, of what breakthrough device or new publication or ministry could better people's lives. Many of us have lots of dreams but find we don't have the combination of opportunity, vision, resources, connections, or persistence to bring to reality what's developing in our heads.

Billy Graham, too, had many limitations of time, energy, and resources, yet somehow he was continually raising his sights, even as he encouraged other entrepreneurs.

Billy became personally engaged with countless ministries, including World Vision, the Salvation Army, Greater Europe Mission, TransWorld Radio, and the Evangelical Council for Financial Accountability.

He helped convene the International Congress on World Evangelization, and helped draft the "Amsterdam Affirmations" that resulted in the Biblical Standards for Evangelists—guidelines that are used to this day.

NO DREAMER IS EVER TOO SMALL;

NO DREAM IS EVER TOO BIG.

Author Unknown

A LEADER: AN INDIVIDUAL WHO
CREATED AN ALCHEMY OF VISION THAT
MOVED PEOPLE FROM WHERE THEY WERE TO
PLACES THAT THEY HAVE NEVER BEEN BEFORE.

Henry Kissinger

MAKE NO LITTLE PLANS.
MAKE THE BIGGEST PLAN YOU CAN THINK OF.

Harry Truman

ATTEMPT GREAT THINGS FOR GOD, EXPECT
GREAT THINGS FROM GOD.

William Carey

An enduring and significant example of Billy's entrepreneurial vision and tenacity was the founding of the magazine *Christianity Today*. Far from a simple journey between two points, the process of creating this new publication involved curves, U-turns, and potholes—and years of hard work.

So how did Billy undertake this giant task and succeed?

First, he listened. He accumulated facts, impressions, insights, and understanding of needs. Filling the mind with these multiple elements brings breakthrough insights and practical concepts. He listened to pastors and Christian leaders during his travels and heard from many of them that there was a true need for this new venture.

Next, he applied his full mental powers. After getting lots of input and counsel from others, and taking time to think through all he had learned, Billy awoke in the night with a rush of detailed ideas. "About two o'clock one night in 1953, an idea raced through my mind, freshly connecting all the things I had seen and pondered about reaching a broader audience....A couple of hours later, the concept of a new magazine was complete. I thought its name should be *Christianity Today*. I worked out descriptions of the various departments, editorial policies, even an estimated budget. I wrote everything I could think of, both about the magazine's organization and about its purpose."

Then, he drove the process. He did the necessary preparatory work by gathering people to help him with his vision, and he sought the money needed.

Billy's father-in-law, Nelson Bell, told the story of traveling with Billy to seek out funds for the new magazine, "On March 10, 1955, we boarded the overnight train from Black Mountain, … for the definitive discussion with J. Howard Pew at Philadelphia whom they hoped would contribute significant funds to the cause. We had a two-berth compartment, and as we neared Philadelphia, Billy said, 'Let's pray.' He got down on the floor, not exactly kneeling but almost as if prostrate before the Lord. I'll never forget that morning on the train."

Nelson Bell told the staff of *Christianity Today* more than ten years later, "I had never seen a man pray like that before exactly. There was an earnestness about his prayers, that the Lord would lead Mr. Pew, if it was the Lord's will, to do something that would insure the beginning of the magazine."

> [Jesus said,] "Ask and it will be given to you; seek and
> you will find; knock and the door will be opened
> to you. For everyone who asks receives; he who seeks
> finds; and to him who knocks, the door will be opened."
>
> MATTHEW 7:7–8

Once the magazine was on the ground running, Billy continued to set up guidelines and structures that would ensure the long-term success of this dream.

Billy made sure to share launch concepts with the staff. He helped shape the tone and content of the magazine with specific insights and article ideas.

Most importantly of all, perhaps, Billy celebrated, prodded, and praised. He was blunt and honest with his criticisms of the magazine's content, but also freely poured on the praise and encouragement. Billy was no mere cheerleader; he was a strategist. He made sure the staff knew exactly what he was thinking, but also how much they were appreciated.

Many times during the past decades when the CTI leadership has faced critical ethical and business decisions, they have asked, "What would Billy do in this situation?" Usually the answers related primarily to moving forward with both love and integrity. Each time the question has been asked, the choice of the road has become clear.

BIRTHING

APPLYING THE PRINCIPLES

Many of us dream about birthing something new, with our personal stamp on it. Just thinking of making such a dream become reality quickens the pulse and stimulates the mind to create scenarios. Resources. Timing. Contacts. Talents. The list of necessities for birthing dreams is long. But sometimes, with vision and persistence, a dream actually becomes a force in the world.

TRADE A PROBLEM FOR A DREAM

Problems come at most of us, often "thick, fast, and furious." We find ourselves enmeshed in them, and any dreams we have fly by as we spend months and years solving old problems. Sometimes we should reprioritize so we can put those dreams front and center. Create something new. Think big. Break out of your ordinary thinking and ordinary tracks!

EXPECT STORMY WEATHER

That's why the new dream can't rely on rookies, no matter how smart or highly motivated. It takes veterans who have been through previous tough times themselves and won't care when thunderheads roll in. Billy knew *Christianity Today* was an important project, so he built a team of strong leaders with deep commitments to see the projects through, no matter what squalls threatened to capsize the boat.

In Filling the Bus, Go With Your Gut

You have to get "the right people on the bus (and the wrong people off the bus)," says writer Jim Collins. To birth a dream takes lots of recruiting skill, and Billy was always a recruiter, connecting with strong people and thinking about how they might best move the cause forward. When *Christianity Today* was in a time of transition and needed a strong, new editor, Billy pursued Dr. Kenneth Kantzer. Ken politely declined the offer, but Billy kept after him, and finally, months later, Ken said yes. Billy had gone with his gut and brought the right person on the bus.

If You Can't Hover, Connect at Important Times of Decision

Leaders positioned to birth dreams know they can't become managers but must hand off those roles. Billy knew he couldn't give all his energies to *Christianity Today* and still fulfill his mission of preaching. But he did make sure to be there for important decisions and in times of need. He personally made sure adequate funding flowed, he helped recruit new leaders, and personally investigated major issues. Long after the birth of a dream, a founder's personal interest can continue to keep it vital and growing.

BE REALISTIC

Especially today, wise leaders must know when to pull the plug on a dream that's in trouble. A failed project must not be allowed to drain the future.

"'In the last days, God says,
I will pour out my Spirit on all people.
Your sons and daughters will prophesy,
your young men will see visions,
your old men will dream dreams.'"
ACTS 2:17

Delight yourself in the LORD
and he will give you the desires of your heart.
Commit your way to the LORD;
trust in him and he will do this:
He will make your righteousness shine like the dawn,
the justice of your cause like the noonday sun.
PSALM 37:4–6

BUILDING BRIDGES

An important part of being a leader is developing relationships outside of your own organization or team. By that measure, Billy Graham was clearly a leader. While he led those inside his organization, his primary efforts were directed outward. Throughout his ministry, he built relational bridges with key individuals whose friendship would prove valuable to the cause. In a world that brings us into contact with all kinds of diversity, the need to build bridges to people beyond our own circles is more vital than ever.

Over the years, Billy's ever-broadening perspective and bridge-building efforts cost him many supporters but won him others. He became a tremendous bridge builder, reaching across denominational, political, racial, and religious boundaries.

Billy's marriage to Ruth was one of his first experiences in building bridges.

Billy Graham had plenty of "natural inclinations" and even prejudices to overcome. After becoming engaged to Ruth, who grew up in the home of Presbyterian missionaries, Billy infuriated her with his stereotypic Baptist suspicion toward establishment denominations. Ruth claims Billy once told her that "Daddy couldn't be in the will of God because he was Presbyterian. I almost gave him his ring back right there."

Billy would later come to deeply trust the counsel of his Presbyterian father-in-law, saying that he "never took a major step without asking his counsel and advice."

As Billy grew, both as a leader and as a man, he worked to build bridges across greater and greater gaps. He began reaching out to other Christian denominations. While still identifying himself as a Baptist, he didn't let his personal preferences stand in the way of positioning his ministry to reach the broadest possible spectrum.

But bridging to other Protestants was just the beginning. It was Billy's reaching out to Catholics that most distinguished his leadership from previous evangelists. He took a bold, almost unprecedented step toward rapprochement with Catholics prior to his 1950 campaign in Boston, a Catholic stronghold. Despite the advice of some of his supporters, Billy sought out Archbishop Richard Cushing's blessing. When reporters asked Cushing what he wanted to tell Catholics about the Graham meetings, he said unambiguously, "Go hear Billy."

Perhaps an even greater divide was spanned by Billy's efforts to connect with the Jewish community. Over the years, Billy found many ways to befriend Jews.

Billy developed a friendship with Rabbi Marc Tanenbaum of the American Jewish Committee, the two of them inviting each other to speak in various venues. In 1977, Billy received the first American Jewish Committee's National Inter-religious Award for his efforts to strengthen "mutual respect and understanding between evangelicals and Jewish communities."

Billy's relationship with Jews took a major hit when, in early 2002, the National Archives released the tape of a conversation recorded in the Oval Office in 1972 between President Nixon and Billy Graham. In an unguarded discussion, Billy made strongly negative comments about Jewish control of media "and what they are doing to this country."

When the tapes were made public, Billy quickly apologized. "My remarks did not reflect my love for the Jewish people," he said. "I humbly ask the Jewish people to reflect on my actions on behalf of Jews over the years that contradict my words in the Oval Office that day."

Billy built bridges not only across denominational and ethnic divides, but also across the gulf between the academic and activist worlds. By personal connections like these, Billy was able to see the larger picture and the various streams of thinking within it. He learned from these giants even as he helped them understand his purpose. Despite the occasional failure, Billy continually worked to bridge all sorts of divides. It's what effective leaders do.

> *Though I am free and belong to no man,*
> *I make myself a slave to everyone, to win as many as*
> *possible. To the Jews I became like a Jew, to win*
> *the Jews. To those under the law I became like one*
> *under the law (though I myself am not under the law),*
> *so as to win those under the law. To those not having*
> *the law I became like one not having the law*
> *(though I am not free from God's law but am under*
> *Christ's law), so as to win those not having the law.*
> *To the weak I became weak, to win the weak. I have*
> *become all things to all men so that by all possible*
> *means I might save some. I do all this for the sake of*
> *the gospel, that I may share in its blessings.*
>
> 1 CORINTHIANS 9:19–23

BRIDGES

APPLYING THE PRINCIPLES

As a boy, Billy took a cat and shut it in the doghouse with the family collie overnight. The next day, the cat and dog came out friends forever. Billy joked, in his autobiography, that the incident may have sown the seeds of his own bridge-building tendencies.

How do you begin to build those connections to people and groups not naturally inclined to work with you?

SHOW INTEREST; ADMIT LIMITATIONS

Bridge building sounds good, but it's almost always humbling. One of the best ways to build bridges is to admit our peculiarities and limitations up front. After all, in most cases they're readily apparent to others anyway.

LEARNING WAS AN INSATIABLE DESIRE WITH
ME. I BURNED TO LEARN, AND I FELT MY
LIMITATIONS OF SCHOOLING AND
BACKGROUND SO TERRIBLY THAT I
DETERMINED TO DO ALL I COULD THROUGH
CONVERSATIONS, PICKING UP EVERYTHING
I COULD FROM EVERYBODY.

Billy Graham

Find Common Ground

How could Billy connect with people in India, Hong Kong, and South Africa? What allowed him to work with Catholics, Jews, conservative Protestants, and intellectuals? He found ways to emphasize their common ground. J. I. Packer, British theologian said, "Billy comes to people not as a visitor from outer space but as a fellow human being. He doesn't come primarily as a Baptist or an American; he comes as a full-grown messenger of the gospel. He has something precious, a message he'd like to share. He's able to communicate in a transcultural way: '*You* have a mind, *you* have a heart, and *you* have a family.' He has a gift for sticking to the main things that apply to all human beings." In establishing a connection with a different sphere, the starting place is not my uniqueness but our common ground.

Build Camaraderie

Every relationship is going to face some seemingly enormous conflicts—different goals, different values, different ways to do things. Bridge building means acknowledging the difficulties and, at the same time, reaffirming your desire not to let them end your relationship.

Cliff Barrows remembers how Billy bridged even potentially tense political divides: "In Budapest during the Cold War, we were sitting across the table from a sharp and intense young man who wanted to tell us how he was converted to communism and why he was motivated by it.

Billy said, 'I'd like to hear that, and then I want to tell you how I was converted to Jesus Christ.' The conversation was wonderful.

The young man said, 'Well, I'd like to convert you to communism.'

And Billy said, 'Thank you. I want to convert you to Jesus Christ.' They shared openly with each other. It was great."

Bridges aren't built by hiding our foundations and intentions but by admitting where we are, respecting those on the other side, and affirming the worth of the connection.

Bring People Together

Bridge building also means emphasizing ways that people can work together, not just work independently. For many of us in leadership, the relationships bridge building produces may turn out to be the most significant thing we accomplish.

If it is possible, as far as it depends on you,
live at peace with everyone.

ROMANS 12:18

May the God who gives endurance and encouragement
give you a spirit of unity among yourselves as you
follow Christ Jesus, so that with one heart and mouth
you may glorify the God and Father of our Lord Jesus
Christ. Accept one another, then, just as Christ
accepted you, in order to bring praise to God.

ROMANS 15:5–7

If you have any encouragement from being united with
Christ, if any comfort from his love, if any fellowship
with the Spirit, if any tenderness and compassion, then
make my joy complete by being like-minded, having
the same love, being one in spirit and purpose.

PHILIPPIANS 2:1–2

IGNITING
OTHER LEADERS

One of the most profound effects of Billy's leadership has been his stoking the fires of other leaders beyond his own organization. He wasn't building his own empire, he was building something bigger.

Many of those heavily influenced by Billy spent little one-on-one time with him. Yet, like many leaders with the same core commitments, Billy demonstrated integrity, wisdom, and a flag others could follow.

> FOLLOW MY EXAMPLE,
> AS I FOLLOW THE EXAMPLE OF CHRIST.
> *The Apostle Paul (1 Corinthians 11:1)*

Pastor Rick Warren has recently been hailed as "America's most influential pastor." Not only did he plant a church twenty years ago that has grown to 21,000 attendees each weekend, but he has written *The Purpose-Driven Life,* a book that has sold over twenty million copies in its first two years, perhaps an all-time record for any book.

When asked if he had observations about the leadership of Billy Graham, Pastor Warren responded immediately, "I'd do anything to honor him; he's had such a profound impact on my life behind the scenes."

So how has Billy Graham influenced Rick Warren and his growing ministry?

"We've pretty much kept our relationship out of the limelight," Rick said, "but he's taught me so much about being a Christian leader and statesman who can cross denominational and international boundaries and serve everybody. My personal goal is to finish the ministry God assigns me in the twenty-first century with the same level of integrity and humility that Billy modeled in the twentieth century.

"When I began Saddleback Church—which I had made a commitment to pastor for the rest of my entire life (I was twenty-five)—I intentionally followed Billy's model of teamwork in selecting guys who would also dedicate the rest of their lives to serving this one church. All of our senior leadership are 'lifers.' We've been together twenty-plus years and have committed to growing old together.

"Much of the growth of Saddleback can be attributed to this team of one mind, one spirit, identical values, close friendship, and personal commitment to each other for life. I get the privilege of serving Christ with my best friends. Billy taught us the value of teamwork."

Billy's ability to inspire other leaders came partly from his desire to learn and grow from others as well. He longed to continue to learn and was generous when it came to others who desired to learn from what he had received.

Billy initiated engagement with multiple generations. His ability to learn from, lock arms with, and inspire leaders who were older or younger or his peers, reveals a fascinating rhythm of leadership effectiveness—starting with Billy's emergence as a young man with much to learn. This ability is a great model for all of us who long to both learn and teach in our position of leadership.

Billy learned from the generation ahead of him, from people like his father-in-law L. Nelson Bell and President Eisenhower.

He maintained vital connections with those in his own generation—learning from people like Robert Evans of Greater Europe Mission and George H. W. Bush.

Billy would then graciously take time to mentor and build relationships with those in the next generation. Says Pastor Leith Anderson, "Billy's willingness to allow others to succeed may be his greatest lasting impact."

Gordon MacDonald is currently editor at large for the journal *Leadership* and chair of World Relief. As pastor of Grace Chapel in Lexington, Massachusetts, he was involved in Billy's New England crusades. Here is Gordon's story of how Billy touched his life when he was just a young leader:

"It was mid-evening, and my wife, Gail, and I were getting settled in our hotel room on the campus of the University of Illinois, where the triennial Urbana Missionary Conference would begin the next day. The year was 1979. There was a knock on the door of our room. Opening the door, I found Billy Graham standing there with a small paper bag in his hand. Handing it to me, he said, 'Here's the medicine I told you about. I went down to a drugstore and got it for you.'

"An hour before, Gail and I had sat at dinner with Billy and others who were to be speakers at the convention. For some reason, I had mentioned that I'd had the flu and that my stomach was still having difficulty digesting food. Billy overheard this and suggested a remedy that could be purchased over the counter at any drugstore. Gail and I made a mental note to look for it the next day."

"Now, an hour later, here's Billy Graham standing at our door with the medicine. I was speechless. All I could finally blurt out was something silly. 'Billy, I can't use that medicine. I'm going to encapsulate it in plastic as a monument to your kindness.'

"I had met Billy Graham on a few previous occasions, but apart from the privilege of shaking his hand, I could hardly claim to know him. Yet here he was, serving the need of a young and somewhat obscure pastor.

"Years later came the most terrible moment of my life. Everything in my life (and Gail's) came to a halt because of my personal failure.

"Billy called me the same day that I stepped down as president of my organization, 'Gordon, this is Billy. I've been trying to call you all morning.' I could hardly speak. He went on, 'I want you to know that you've already been forgiven by God, and that I forgive you.'

"As far as I can remember, this was the first word of forgiveness spoken by anyone except Gail. I wept. How had this man heard of my situation so quickly, and why would he take the time to call and offer this hopeful word?

"After several more minutes of conversation, he concluded the call saying, 'Why don't you move down here to Montreat for a year or so and help me write sermons?' I could not imagine this happening, but the very fact that Billy would say this brought a ray of sunlight into that darkness. What a creative way to say that there just might be a tomorrow."

IGNITING LEADERS

APPLYING THE PRINCIPLES

Evangelist Leighton Ford was mentored by Billy, starting when he was in high school. Now, Leighton has a special passion for mentoring young people who are becoming the new generation of leaders. He spills out a steady flow of practical and thoughtful insights on empowering young leaders. Here are a few of them:

CHOOSE A FEW WISELY; SHARE OPENLY OVER THE LONG HAUL

We can attempt to encourage many, and in life's ordinary flow, the small gesture and the caring word can raise sights and empower, but we can make the deepest impact by investing more heavily in a few. Leighton says, "Long-term tracking of people is very important. To be a 'spiritual director' is to help someone remember their song when they've forgotten it." When you've been with someone over ten years, you see the ups and downs and can help them stay in tune."

Entrust the Trustworthy

Billy took a chance on Leighton when he was only twenty-three, asking him to take charge of church relations for his meetings in New York. Entrusting someone with large responsibilities always includes taking a chance, and especially with young aspirants who have no track record. Yet the principle is clear: to grow and be stretched, the leaders of tomorrow must be given significant responsibilities today.

Calling the Twelve to him, [Jesus] sent them out two by two and gave them authority over evil spirits. These were his instructions: "Take nothing for the journey except a staff—no bread, no bag, no money in your belts. Wear sandals but not an extra tunic. Whenever you enter a house, stay there until you leave that town. And if any place will not welcome you or listen to you, shake the dust off your feet when you leave, as a testimony against them." They went out and preached that people should repent. They drove out many demons and anointed many sick people with oil and healed them.

MARK 6:7–13

Look Down the Road

Emerging leaders don't stay static; they need to be empowered in changing dynamics, and this necessitates fresh thinking.

Leighton remembers that after eight years of working with Billy, he called him up to his home one day and said, "Leighton, I've been thinking and praying about this. I think you ought to develop your own team and go to Canada, your native country, and evangelize across Canada. We'll support you if you want to start your own organization, or you can be part of our organization.

"He saw at that point, I think, that I shouldn't just stay 'under his wing' but to move out on my own. He encouraged me to do that, and it was a very major thing.

"Perhaps he saw I had potential to be more than an assistant to him; maybe it was for both my sake and to avoid possible conflict down the years—if I grew impatient with a lack of scope. It was a lot of foresight on his part."

LEADERSHIP IS STIRRING PEOPLE SO THEY
ARE MOVED FROM INSIDE THEMSELVES.

Frederick R. Kappel

THE FINAL TEST OF A LEADER IS THAT HE
LEAVES BEHIND IN OTHERS THE CONVICTION
AND THE WILL TO CARRY ON.

Walter Lippmann

YOU MUST BE CAREFUL HOW YOU WALK,
AND WHERE YOU GO, FOR THERE ARE THOSE
FOLLOWING YOU WHO WILL SET
THEIR FEET WHERE YOURS ARE SET.

Robert E. Lee

NOT THE CRY, BUT THE
FLIGHT OF THE WILD DUCK,
LEADS THE FLOCK TO FLY AND FOLLOW.

Chinese Proverb

SOWING SEEDS
IN ALL SEASONS

Leaders cannot avoid it. For good or ill, they are sowing seeds everywhere they go, in everything they do. A leader's every action has consequences both intended and unintended.

People are like plowed ground; seeds find the soil of minds and emotions, sprouting powerful changes. Who knows the results? Tiny seeds can produce sturdy trees or nourishing grains or delicate flowers.

We all know, however, that sowing good seed is often hard, tedious work. We may long to escape the necessity of always being "on," of day after day, year after year following through on all our commitments to those who look at our every word and action.

At times, we simply want to escape.

However, there's a far better solution—*recovery*.

We are invited to serve with energy and joy, and that means a rhythm of hard work, yes, but also the laughter of friends and the recharging from solitude, and, most of all, the empowering of consistently being true to our deepest values and commitments.

During his many decades of struggling with the weight of his fame, Billy kept working at what people today call self-management. And he kept sowing seeds consistently, on vacation or off, in settings both formal and casual, taking action and speaking to others in ways resonant with his convictions. The apostle Paul said that he was prepared "in season and out of season." So was Billy.

Sowing good seeds all the time results in surprises that may astound the sower. Seeds take root and grow into unexpected new realities.

The following are just two of the many stories of how the seeds that Billy sowed have had a greater impact than he, or anyone, ever could have imagined.

SPARKING A CHANGE OF HEART

Casual interaction in a family and a gracious giving of his time to one young man had larger ramifications than anyone would have thought at the time. In the summer of 1985, the family of then Vice President Bush invited Billy Graham to be their weekend guest in Kennebunkport, Maine.

George H. W. Bush gathered the younger Bushes around the fireplace with Billy and suggested they should talk about spiritual issues and ask questions. The younger George Bush had been struggling with his drinking problem. His being together with Billy was to have a profound effect.

"What he said sparked a change in my heart," George W. Bush has explained. "I don't remember the exact words. It was more the power of his example. The Lord was so clearly reflected in his gentle and loving demeanor. The next day we walked and talked at Walker's Point, and I knew I was in the presence of a great man. He was like a magnet; I felt drawn to seek something different. He didn't lecture or admonish; he shared warmth and concern. Billy Graham didn't make you feel guilty; he made you feel loved."

During that conversation, Billy turned to Bush and said, "Are you right with God?"

"No," Bush replied, "but I want to be."

That encounter, while not producing instantaneous change, did nevertheless have a lingering effect.

"Over the course of that weekend," said Bush, "Billy Graham planted a mustard seed in my soul, a seed that grew over the next year. He led me to the path, and I began walking. It was the beginning of a change in my life. I had always been a 'religious' person, had regularly attended church, but that weekend my faith took on a new meaning. It was the beginning of a new walk where I would commit my heart to Jesus Christ."

Years later, when he had ascended to the presidency, Bush asked some religious leaders to pray for him by saying, "You know, I had a drinking problem. Right now I should be in a bar in Texas, not the Oval Office. There is only one reason that I am in the Oval Office and not in a bar. I found faith. I found God. I am here because of the power of prayer."

A Chance Meeting

"As a new Christian working at a hotel," says Mark Driscoll, "I once had the privilege of chatting for about ten minutes with Billy Graham, who was staying there as a guest. He was sitting in the restaurant by himself, wearing a Minnesota Twins baseball cap, reading the paper and eating breakfast when I approached him to introduce myself. He asked if I knew the Lord, and I explained that I was a new Christian and that God had called me into ministry. His words were very encouraging, and he kindly promised to pray for me.

"After our informal conversation ended, other people seated around him in the restaurant recognized who he was. Rather than rushing off to avoid being bothered, Dr. Graham graciously stayed in the restaurant to visit with people, share the gospel, and pray over the children who came to sit upon his lap and have their picture taken with him as if he were Santa Claus. His gracious spirit and humble approachability made a great impression upon many of the non-Christians I worked with. To this day I sincerely thank God for working through Billy Graham in such a wonderfully faithful manner, both in and out of the pulpit."

Mark Driscoll went on to plant Mars Hill Church in Seattle and to form an entire church-planting network, Acts 29, which by 2004 had launched more than a hundred churches.

Be prepared in season and out of season;
correct, rebuke and encourage—
with great patience and careful instruction.

2 TIMOTHY 4:2

He who goes out weeping,
*   carrying seed to sow,*
will return with songs of joy,
*   carrying sheaves with him.*

PSALM 126:6

Sow your seed in the morning,
*   and at evening let not your hands be idle,*
for you do not know which will succeed,
*   whether this or that,*
*   or whether both will do equally well.*

ECCLESIASTES 11:6

[God] who supplies seed to the sower and bread for
food will also supply and increase your store of seed and
*   will enlarge the harvest of your righteousness.*

2 CORINTHIANS 9:10

LEADERSHIP LESSONS:

SOWING

APPLYING THE PRINCIPLES

Sometimes we may feel our particular gifts are ordinary seeds with little potential for significant fruit. Yet as we refine our skills and grow as leaders, each of us might be amazed at how our uniqueness unexpectedly teaches and inspires others.

APPLY YOUR GIFTEDNESS WITH GREAT EXPECTATION

Having "great expectations" about multiple effects of our leadership is not unrealistic. In fact, expectations are often a major factor in sowing seeds that produce great results. It was often said about Billy Graham that he had "great expectations." He, in turn, was often amazed at the many unanticipated results of his efforts and prayers.

PRIORITIZE SELF-MANAGEMENT

Being an effective leader requires not just skills and focus but also attention to your own heart and soul. We may object that it's self-centered to spend all that time on ourselves. However, it's essential we prioritize our own physical, psychological, and spiritual vitality.

Above all else, guard your heart,
*   for it is the wellspring of life.*
        PROVERBS 4:23

DON'T STEP ON A GREEN SHOOT

When we are "established," we sometimes don't realize the power we have, and the impact of our smallest action.

Harry Truman didn't make that mistake. He understood

the weight of his words. Once, as he took questions from an audience, he had to respond negatively to a high school boy. After the meeting was over, he had the Secret Service bring the boy to him to reassure him. Truman said he hadn't wanted that boy to go through his life with the reputation that he had been put down by the president of the United States. Truman understood that his feet could be like giant boots crushing green shoots. We, in turn, may not be president, but each of our boots may seem large, indeed, to many of those we lead.

A bruised reed he will not break,
and a smoldering wick he will not snuff out.
MATTHEW 12:20

TOUCH OTHERS—WITH AWE AT YOUR POWERS

When we have good seed to sow, seeing it grow is an awesome thing. When we lead others, we have powers that should fill us with awe and a sense of deep responsibility. The touch of a leader radiates power, for good or for ill. We're usually unaware of the power we possess. It may be a power that affects very few, but to those few, a touch can be decisive. Sowing seeds in all seasons is more than planting words or concepts or driving a process. It's consistently sowing with a sense of great responsibility and of great possibilities.

PART SIX

DEEPENING *in* EVERY DECADE

Some leaders as they age draw back and start to calcify. Others keep growing and maintain their power.

Billy kept developing, not only as a person but as a leader in a dramatically changing world, by continually plugging into voltage outside of himself, by leveraging his weaknesses, innovating, and always leading with love, which he unceasingly made the driving force of his ministry and life.

LEARNING—AND
LEVERAGING WEAKNESS

Great strengths are usually accompanied by significant weaknesses. Great leaders accept their weaknesses and leverage them. First they admit them, then adapt, delegate, and constantly learn.

Billy Graham, despite his preaching to millions, has often professed he wasn't a great preacher. It's true that others were more eloquent. Yet this drove him to concentrate on the essentials and to depend not on his own skills, but the Spirit. Billy had not only innate intuitions but understood that others had insights to share. He knew how much he needed those insights, and he knew how getting them would connect him with others. Therefore, he consistently set himself up to learn from everyone.

Billy's brother Melvin tells the story of how, even as he was beginning to gain a national reputation, Billy still saw the importance of learning from people of all walks of life. He humbly submitted himself to the teaching of others who had the wisdom of life experience.

"There was a fella named Bill Henderson, had a little grocery store in the black section of Charlotte—just a run-down little dump of a place. He was a tiny fella. He had long sleeves that came way down, and he wore a tie that would hang down below his waist. But I tell you, that little old man, he knew the Bible!

"This was probably the late forties," Melvin explained, "and Billy had been around a lot of places."

This was when Billy was United Airlines' top traveler and had preached in many European cities.

Melvin wagged his head in wonder. "Henderson barely made a living. It was a place the black people would come to get chewing tobacco and stuff like that. Most black people loved him, but that little man got beat up on many times, got his store robbed time and time again, but he just loved the Lord. I mean, he just *loved* God. Billy loved to hear Bill Henderson tell him about the Scriptures. He lived them; it wasn't weekend Christianity. And he could pray. He'd pray for Billy and his young ministry. And he witnessed all the time.

"In the afternoons Billy would go there and just sit and talk to him. He'd sit on an old crate—I don't think they had a chair in the place—and let Bill teach him."

The young Billy Graham, fresh from air travel all over the country to address large audiences, took the time to sit on a crate to learn from a humble, authentic witness in the trenches. The image blends with his constant learning from executives, professors, pastors, presidents—and his candid, well-read wife. Over and over again people say about Billy that "he was always learning, always teachable."

Billy was always quick to learn from anyone with a better idea or a better method. He also learned from his critics. One writer castigated him for a statement that was seen as insensitive to the poor. Graham wrote him an apology and urged him to "kick me in the pants" when necessary—and thereafter he watched what he said.

Even Billy's "weakness" of waffling on certain difficult decisions because he didn't want to say no, and his not wanting to fire anyone, was leveraged into strength— because he was ever the humble learner, giving strong colleagues their freedom and passionately driving toward the best win-win approach. For instance, he knew that if you don't feel called to play the role of "bad cop," you have to find someone who could.

Billy accepted his weaknesses, leveraging them and keeping his eyes on the goal.

Joni Eareckson Tada, who was paralyzed from a diving accident when she was a teenager, has been an outstanding leader herself, despite her dramatic limitations. She has often appeared with Billy. We found her insights about leveraging weaknesses especially insightful as she told us about her experience at Graham's Moscow crusade in the early 1990s:

"My translator was Oleg, a young Russian man who was severely visually impaired. He commented while we were on the platform, 'Joni, isn't it wonderful that God is using me, a blind boy, and you, a paralyzed woman to reach the people in my nation?' I got a lump in my throat, just thinking of his point: that God delights in choosing weak people to accomplish his work.

"I was about to respond to Oleg when I saw Billy Graham slowly rise (with a little help) from his seat to walk to the platform. It was around the time he had received an initial diagnosis of Parkinson's disease. As I watched Mr. Graham steady himself to step up to the pulpit, I said to Oleg, 'Friend, God is using not only a blind boy and a paralyzed woman but an elderly man on shaky legs to reach your people!'"

How did Billy react when she shared those thoughts with him? "He wasn't embarrassed. This is what has inspired me most about this extraordinary leader. Not only does he keep moving ahead, despite his physical challenges, he seems to boast in them.

"Mr. Graham is keenly aware that God's power always shows up best in weakness," said Joni. "This is why he inspires me with my own disability of thirty-seven years. His example of perseverance under pressure speaks volumes to me and to many others. Mr. Graham knows God's heart when it comes to the lowly and needy. He reflects this through his own humility, and he lives it daily."

> *[Jesus] said…, "My grace is sufficient for you,*
> *for my power is made perfect in weakness."*
>
> 2 Corinthians 12:9

LEVERAGING WEAKNESS

APPLYING THE PRINCIPLES

Today's leaders are entering a rapidly changing world.
The ability to learn as we go and leverage weaknesses
may be tomorrow's most important leadership skill.

COMPENSATE, AND DODGE DISASTER

As a result of remaining conscious of his own weaknesses
and the potential for failure, Billy continually sought to
compensate for his own shortcomings.

Interestingly, the most effective way to do that is not
to bemoan our own limitations. It's just the opposite: it's
to eagerly and happily glean from the strengths that
others offer.

LISTEN INTENTLY

"I remind myself every morning: nothing I say this day
will teach me anything. So if I'm going to learn, I must
do it by listening," said Larry King, the famous
interviewer and a close friend of Billy Graham. Billy
certainly shared that trait with his friend. Graham
biographer William Martin said listening was one of

Billy's great strengths. "He never hardened into the place where he assumed, 'Here I am. I'm Billy Graham, and you and your ideas can bounce up against me.' No, he was always willing to grow, like a ripple that is constantly moving outward in an ever-growing circle."

Roald Amundsen was a national hero in his native Norway. He gained worldwide acclaim as an explorer in being the first person to reach the South Pole and the first to touch both poles in a single lifetime.

Amundsen's great gift "was a willingness to learn from those around him." In 1903, Amundsen was on the way to becoming the first person to navigate the Northwest Passage between the Canadian mainland and its Arctic Islands. He became fascinated with the Netsilik, an isolated group of Eskimos, and he lived as they lived: "He careened down hills in the dog sleds, slept in their igloos, and adopted their reindeer-fur dress."

What he learned from these unlikely educators eventually proved strategic in Amundsen's ultimately successful attempt to reach the South Pole. Learning from unlikely sources made the difference between success and failure, life and death.

Repristinate!

Sometimes a leader is charged with protecting a certain asset—whether an endowment, a tradition, or an institution. But even the task of preservation demands learning and growth.

In his book on leadership, *Certain Trumpets*, Garry Wills points out that in order for a tradition to be worth passing on to another generation, you must repristinate it, make it pristine again—"restore it to its original state or condition."

This is what Billy Graham was doing by his habit of asking people to teach him. He was repristinating his relationships and his understanding.

LEARNING IS NOT ATTAINED BY CHANCE.
IT MUST BE SOUGHT FOR WITH ARDOR.

Abigail Adams

I will listen to what God the LORD will say;
he promises peace to his people, his saints.
PSALM 85:8

I LIKE TO LISTEN. I HAVE LEARNED
A GREAT DEAL FROM LISTENING CAREFULLY.
MOST PEOPLE NEVER LISTEN.

Ernest Hemingway

Let the wise listen and add to their learning,
and let the discerning get guidance.
PROVERBS 1:5

Jesus said…, "Take my yoke upon you and learn from
me, for I am gentle and humble in heart, and you will
find rest for your souls."
MATTHEW 11:25, 29

PLUGGING INTO
CONTINUOUS VOLTAGE

Billy's colleagues often speak of the constant pressure Billy has always felt. It's easy to see why.

Imagine the pressure of conducting the funeral for the disgraced former President Richard Nixon while the nation skeptically watched and listened for every nuance.

Imagine the emotional demands on him when he conducted the memorial service after the Oklahoma City bombing.

The service at the National Cathedral right after the 9/11 attacks on the World Trade Center and the Pentagon presented perhaps the greatest pressure of all.

But Billy found the inner resources to rise to each of these momentous occasions.

How could he maintain his strength and sense of commitment, not only in his last decades but throughout the unrelenting pressure of the leadership marathon he has run for sixty years?

Billy has not been impervious to the pressures; his body and psyche have paid a steep price. But he has taken his own advice, so often expressed in various ways in his newspaper columns, books, and articles. He has continually plugged himself into the spiritual and psychological voltage that has made this half-century saga possible.

From the beginning, his spiritual power has come from prayer and the Bible. He spent large amounts of time connecting with his source of wisdom, cleansing, and power.

O God, you are my God,
*   earnestly I seek you;*
my soul thirsts for you,
*   my body longs for you,*
in a dry and weary land
*   where there is no water.*
I have seen you in the sanctuary
*   and beheld your power and your glory.*
Because your love is better than life,
*   my lips will glorify you.*
I will praise you as long as I live,
*   and in your name I will lift up my hands.*

PSALM 63:1–4

Despite the sense of being physically drained and empty at times, throughout the years Billy didn't quit. As Grady Wilson observed, "When he mounts the platform, though, it seems the Holy Spirit gives him a resurgence of vitality and power."

Pastor Warren Wiersbe offered us similar testimony. "When Billy stood up to speak one night, I thought, *This guy is not going to make it.* You could tell he was not at his best physically; he just didn't look like he was up to it. And then something happened, like you plugged in a computer—that power was there. The minute he stepped into that pulpit and opened his Bible, something happened. I've heard him say that when he gets up to preach, he feels like electricity is going through him."

This is the picture so often described by his colleagues: weakness drawing on the Spirit. And it wasn't simply physical fatigue but a wrestling with the realities of the human condition and his own shortcomings.

For Christ's sake, I delight in weaknesses,
in insults, in hardships, in persecutions, in difficulties.
For when I am weak, then I am strong.

2 CORINTHIANS 12:10

Throughout his long life of ministry, Billy has found that he must constantly return to the Source. "Every time I give an invitation, I am in an attitude of prayer," he says. "I feel emotionally, physically, and spiritually drained. It becomes a spiritual battle of such proportions that sometimes I feel faint. There is an inward groaning and agonizing in prayer that I cannot possibly put into words."

The Spirit helps us in our weakness. We do not know
what we ought to pray for, but the Spirit himself
intercedes for us with groans that words cannot express.
And he who searches our hearts knows the mind
of the Spirit, because the Spirit
intercedes for the saints in accordance with God's will.
ROMANS 8:26–27

CONTINUOUS VOLTAGE

APPLYING THE PRINCIPLES

When you purchase a computer, you get an owner's manual and usually a troubleshooting guide. Almost invariably, the first instruction is, "Make sure the computer is plugged into the power source."

It's an obvious necessity, but in life and leadership, that elementary step is often overlooked. Leaders must be aware of what fuels them. Sometimes they become so focused on their objectives, so driven to accomplish, that they don't notice a power outage.

Jesus said, "What good is it for a man to gain the whole world, yet forfeit his soul?" (Mark 8:36). Most leaders know the all-consuming demands that come with leadership. Yet without attention to our souls, our greatest human efforts eventually sputter out.

RECOGNIZE THAT SPIRITUAL HEALTH ISN'T AUTOMATIC

Mindy Caliguire worked for several years in a marketing firm; now she helps leaders with "spiritual formation." She understands that keeping spiritually healthy amid the demands of leadership isn't easy. Here's how she communicated that to a group of leaders. "What tends to emerge in the life of a person who neglects their soul?" she asked them.

"Somebody ventured, '*anxiety.*' They called out *self-absorption, shame, apathy, toxic anger, chronic fatigue, lack of confidence, isolation, no compassion, self-oriented, drivenness, loss of vision.*

"Then, I asked the opposite: 'What emerges in your life when your soul is healthy? When you're connected with God?'

"*Love, joy, compassion, generosity of spirit, peace, ability to trust, discernment.* Heads nodded in acknowledgment as individuals recalled seasons of life when this was their experience. *Boundlessness, creativity, vision, balance, focus.* All in all, a pretty desirable list."

Then Mindy pointed out that every day, each of us is voting for one or the other of these two lists.

Deepen a Dry Well

Bill Leslie was an inner-city pastor and community organizer. We talked to him shortly before his sudden and unexpected death several years ago. We asked him about the spiritual power needed to be a community leader in a tough neighborhood in Chicago.

He told us that over the years, he felt continuously worn down in his efforts to alleviate suffering, fight poverty, and persevere despite the crime and violence that permeated his neighborhood. One day, when discouragement and conflict caused him to hit bottom, he made an appointment with a nun, Ann Wilder, who had been recommended to him as a wise counselor and spiritual director.

"The real problem is that you are like a hand pump whose pipe isn't deep enough," Ann said. "You're pumping surface water, so by 10:30 in the morning, they've pumped you dry. Deep down there are underground streams. If you can get your pipe down there, there's so much water that no matter how much anyone pumps out of you, they'll have a hard time lowering the level of the water even one inch."

Ann winked and added, "I guess what I'm really saying to you, Bill, is that you need a personal relationship with Jesus Christ."

Bill laughed, because as an evangelical Christian, he figured he was the one who was supposed to be saying that to the nun. He told us, "She knew I had a relationship with Jesus but was trying to say, 'Way down deep, you're shallow!'"

Ann helped him by regularly pointing him back to his spiritual source, encouraging him to pay attention to his physical health, and develop some key friendships. Bill was then able to continue to effectively lead without consuming himself.

Trust the Power Given

Because Billy realized the power didn't come *from* him but came *through* him, he didn't feel obligated to overreach with his methods. That confidence in the power of the message frees the leader from having to over work on presentation techniques to convince the listeners. Likewise, people can sense that efforts are forced when a leader isn't convinced his message is sound. Because Billy was well connected to his continuous voltage, he knew where the power came from. He simply made himself available to receive it.

God, who said, "Let light shine out of darkness,"
made his light shine in our hearts to give us the light of
the knowledge of the glory of God in the face of Christ.
But we have this treasure in jars of clay to show that
this all-surpassing power is from God and not from us.

2 Corinthians 4:6–7

Develop Voltage-Producing Friendships

John Wesley used the term *conferencing* to describe the kinds of thoughtful reflection and interaction with others that can deepen and keep current our spiritual lives.

Robert Cooley former president of Gordon-Conwell Seminary talked about Billy's influence on him in learning the importance of "conferencing."

"He emphasized strongly the importance of a life of prayer and spiritual formation in leading the seminary. He kept saying, 'I know how much you're going to have to depend upon this.' I immediately established the discipline of daily prayer in the president's office. I invited everyone and anyone who would join me for prayer. I had one professor, J. Christy Wilson, who never missed a day during his time at the seminary in joining me. It was the discipline of committing to prayer, sharing needs, concerns, and praise. Those were essential disciplines that I tried to not just model but to make integral to my daily life.

"It created more joy within. You can easily get entrapped in the wake of the day's programs and concerns leading an organization—no wonder the word *burden* comes to mind. The weight of the issues can rob you of your joy. But prayer teaches you that rejoicing becomes an activity. It's more than a feeling. It's a discipline. It's a daily thing."

INNOVATING

Continual change is the reality of our era. Effective leaders must blend history and precedent with wisdom from the past, applying them to emerging realities.

Billy Graham launched his ministry in an era when many religious leaders warned that Christianity would survive only by "modernizing" its message. Yet he stubbornly preached historical, biblical Christianity. At the same time, he communicated this message innovatively. Billy may have drawn from the organizing genius of Dwight Moody and the preaching dynamics of Billy Sunday, but he used communication tools as they emerged, keeping the message the same, but adapting to the delivery systems.

This spirit continued throughout his career.

Why the strong motivation to innovate? Billy's associates insist his drive to innovate was rooted in his calling to reach out to others with God's love.

What else, they ask, could motivate him in the 1960s to don sunglasses, shabby clothes, and a baseball cap to mingle in New York City among protesters of Students for a Democratic Society?

Why else would he walk into a music store, load up on rock albums, and then sit down at his Montreat home to hear an unfamiliar generation's coming-of-age anthems?

Graham left his generational comfort zone because he believed in his message and loved those who needed to hear it.

Generational changes often catch leaders unaware, and Billy's sensitivities did not ensure against that. Rick Marshall noticed in the late 1980s a developing generational disconnect. As director of Billy's campaigns, he relied on the support of local ministers, who began hinting to Marshall that evangelism meetings had run their course.

Marshall knew the campaign programming had become dated, so imagine his concern when the cochairmen of Billy's 1994 Cleveland campaign—businessman Gordon Heffern and former Cleveland Indians all-star Andre Thornton—asked him how the BGEA would help them reach Ohio's youth. "I was stunned. Privately I thought, *I don't think we can do that because I've been watching over the last several years, and the kids aren't coming.*"

Spurred on by Heffern and Thornton's challenge, Marshall brainstormed ways to encourage youth to come hear Billy. He created plans for flashy visual presentations and edgy rock music. Marshall took his plan straight to the CEO. "I got Mr. Graham on the phone and shared with him the vision."

"You know what he said? 'That's nothing. Let me tell you about what we used to do.' And he went all the way back into the 1940s and told me about the Youth for Christ rallies: horses on the stage tapping out answers to Bible questions; a hundred pianos in the middle of football fields; crazy, wild clothing and ties with bright lights hooked up to battery packs."

With Billy's blessing, Marshall booked two of the most prominent Christian music acts—dc Talk and Michael W. Smith—and developed a youth-focused advertising campaign to broadcast on rock radio and local television stations. At 4:00 P.M., before the debut of Billy's reinvented youth night, 35,000 kids eagerly waited for the stadium gates to open. When the festivities finally began at 7:00 P.M., 65,000 youth screamed for their favorite musicians first, then listened intently to Billy.

"I learned something about change," Rick said. "While there's a lot of discussion about change and the necessity of it, I discovered through my dialogue with Billy that change is not about the head—it's about the heart. When the heart is soft, the mind is open to change at any age."

INNOVATING

APPLYING THE PRINCIPLES

Every leader has always had to innovate. People change or die, resources expand or dry up, someone gets an idea that catches fire and changes the chemistry. Adapting to new realities and bringing experience to bear is what leadership is all about.

Keep Progress in Perspective

Wherever we find ourselves on the spectrum, from early adapters to wary veterans, we do well to adjust our personal enthusiasms or cautions to the realities at hand. Doing that takes broad perspective beyond our personal experiences. The more we know, the more we can apply. We need to learn about lots of different ways of thinking so that our innovations will meet people's needs and not just our own personal passions.

> *Each of you should look not only to your own interests,*
> *but also to the interests of others.*
> PHILIPPIANS 2:4

Find Innovators

To innovate takes innovators—people who have open minds, creativity, and drive. In any field, a leader pressing for innovation needs an abundance of talent: people who have the ability to adapt and seek new solutions. Creating an environment of innovation and creativity is a matter of insight, determination, and communication.

What sort of environment? The old clichés still work:

Employ the cutting edge of technology, not the bleeding edge. (Don't adapt *too* early.)

Think outside of the box. (Constantly stretch your imaginations and continue to learn and grow.)

Dismount dead horses. (This one sounds so easy—who keeps riding a dead horse? But when you've invested money and passion into something and people are producing it regularly, it's very hard to declare it dead and get out of the saddle.)

Be Quick—But Realistic

"The bearing of a child takes nine months, no matter how many women are assigned."

What an apt metaphor for any process of innovation! Every adaptive step forward involves not just the bright idea but also its refinement, buy-in by others, and its development and application. Fit the pace and the process to the project.

Innovation by its nature is messy. So is working with people. That's why realism about pace and progress is crucial.

Lighten Up

Injecting a light touch can put the frustrations natural to innovation in perspective. For instance, Harry Truman insisted on honest government and realistic adaptation. On meeting resistance to some of his initiatives, he had a humorous response. At that time, the Floogie Bird was a toy made to fly only backwards. He made it famous by seizing on this fact and dubbing his critics "Floogie Birds." He puckishly described them as resisting progress, wanting to fly only backwards.

The Graham team, as noted, was well-known for appropriate humor. Like condiments, a light touch often makes experiences more palatable.

UNABASHEDLY GROPE

The innovative process is far from straightforward business analysis, audience research, application, and rollout. Sometimes it is much more like groping in a dark room for a door handle.

Sometimes a solution is so simple that we ask,

"Why couldn't we have come up with this four meetings ago? Why did we need to grope through all this analysis and dialogue?"

But even the geniuses among us have been known to make their biggest discoveries by feeling around in the dark. Albert Einstein said, "How do I do my work? I grope."

The innovations most of us try to develop fall far short of breakthroughs in nuclear physics. But all of us, at times, have to dig deeply when we don't see the immediate solution to the problem.

YOU CAN JUDGE YOUR AGE BY THE
AMOUNT OF PAIN YOU FEEL WHEN YOU COME
INTO CONTACT WITH A NEW IDEA.

John Nuveen

GEARED TO THE TIMES,
ANCHORED TO THE ROCK.

Youth for Christ's motto

I AM SELLING THE GREATEST
PRODUCT IN THE WORLD. WHY SHOULDN'T IT
BE PROMOTED AS WELL AS SOAP?

Billy Graham

"Forget the former things;
do not dwell on the past.
See, I am doing a new thing!
Now it springs up; do you not perceive it?
I am making a way in the desert
and streams in the wasteland," [says the Lord.]

ISAIAH 43:18–19

LEADING WITH LOVE

When asked, "What would you say is the bottom line distinctive of Billy's leadership?" John Corts, a key employee of Billy's organization for thirty-five years, said, "Love. The difference between him and so many other leaders is that whatever the circumstances, Billy always led with love."

Billy Graham often quoted the Bible's familiar words, "For God so loved the world that he gave his only Son," as well as Scripture's profound assertion, "God is love." Yet how did this belief permeate his leadership and actually impact people? How did he balance this with the leader's necessity to face brutal facts and take action on them, and to deal with life's rugged realities?

Somehow, in the most difficult situations, Billy has communicated a heart full of love for others. People sense it. His internalizing love has deepened through the years as he has listened intently to the Spirit, whose first fruit the Bible says is love.

Two years after 9/11, with its destruction of the World Trade Center, Billy was holding meetings in Dallas. Some Americans felt all Muslims were suspect. Billy's colleague, Rick Marshall, told us, "It surprised me to learn that one of the largest U.S. populations of Muslims is in central Texas. Billy did an interview with the *Dallas Morning News*, and one of the questions the writer put to him was, 'Dr. Graham, do you have a message for the Muslims of Texas?' He answered without hesitation.

"The next day the headline on the front page, bottom section was 'Billy Graham has a message for Muslims: God loves them, and I love them.'

"It was a powerful statement. Talk about cutting right to the heart of the gospel! Everyone was talking about it, because it defused so much anger and so much criticism. It brought to the table the hallmark of Billy's ministry."

When Hugh Downs interviewed Billy on the *20/20* television program, the subject turned to homosexuality.

Hugh looked directly at Billy and asked, "If you had a homosexual child, would you love him?"

Billy didn't miss a beat. He answered gently, "Why, I would love that one even more."

Jesus said to his followers as he was about to leave them: "I will be with you only a little longer. A new commandment I give you: Love one another. As I have loved you, so you must love one another."

Billy has taken this command from his Leader very seriously. To many ears, the fact that Billy would call employees like Sherwood Wirt "beloved" sounds strangely foreign. But the word not only comes from the Bible, it was what Billy felt toward his fellow disciples and what he determined to make central in his life.

How far should love extend? Jesus said we must love our enemies. To genuinely love a vicious enemy would take supernatural power. The Bible's original Greek uses *agape* to describe exactly that—supernatural love that transcends human capacities.

Martin Luther King Jr., in leading the Civil Rights Movement, advocated…the transforming power of love.

King explained what the Bible's word means when facing rough realities: "*Agape* is disinterested love.… *Agape* does not begin by discriminating between worthy and unworthy people, or any qualities people possess.

It begins by loving others *for their sakes*…therefore *agape* makes no distinction between friend and enemy; it is directed toward both."

So Billy showed love, even to his most savage critics and to those who had hurt him the most. He was moved by compassion for those who suffer or have no hope, his love extending to Christian, Muslim, Hindu, agnostic, or atheist. That's what *agape* required of him.

Yet for all Billy's kindness and compassion, he felt the normal human emotions. At times, he was confronted with situations requiring more than compassion.

For instance, John Akers told us that although Billy could usually disarm hostile situations, sometimes he was forced to be stern. "He was in Communist East Germany to speak to a Lutheran synod," John told us. "The reception was so cold, the conveners so arrogant, that when he got up he said, 'When I came in, I had seldom met such a hostile group, and it shouldn't be that way. We are brothers in Christ, and I love you. But this atmosphere does not reflect that.'"

John remembers that Billy's forthright statements "just wiped them out." They got the message— sometimes "tough love" requires redemptive correction.

Disgraced televangelist Jim Bakker also testifies to the love of Billy Graham and his family. Despite the fact that Bakker's public scandal had brought suspicion and scorn on all evangelists, the Grahams maintained a friendship with Bakker throughout his imprisonment and afterward.

"The first Sunday out," Bakker said, "Ruth Graham called the halfway house I was living in and asked permission for me to go to church with her that Sunday morning. When I got there, the pastor welcomed me and sat me with the Graham family. There were like two whole rows of them—I think every Graham aunt and uncle and cousin was there. The organ began playing and the place was full, except for a seat next to me. Then the doors opened and in walked Ruth Graham. She walked down that aisle and sat next to inmate 07407–059. I had only been out of prison forty-eight hours, but she told the world that morning that Jim Bakker was her friend."

LOVE

APPLYING THE PRINCIPLES

When we consider Billy's love toward so many—and his colleagues' frequent assertions that it was Billy's spirit of love that bonded them to him and radiated out to others—we understand how essential love was to his leadership.

Yet what about us? Can we—should we—apply this to our own leadership? The implications may feel overwhelming.

With all the pressures and urgencies thrust upon him, Billy knew that leading with love was beyond his human capacities. But that was the point. He could in weakness become a conduit for a greater force. And in spite of our own weaknesses and limitations, God can enable us to want to lead others with his amazing love.

Among the greatest expressions of all literature is the soaring pinnacle of the apostle Paul's writing, the love chapter of 1 Corinthians 13. It calls for the *agape* love Martin Luther King Jr. spoke about.

To apply it to our own challenges, we can read it this way:

If I lead others like an angel from God,
but have not love,
I am a clanging cymbal.

Love is patient; love is kind.
Love doesn't envy.
Love does not boast, is not proud.
Love is not self-seeking.
Love is not easily angered; it keeps no record of wrongs.

So there remain many essential elements of leadership,
among them, courage, humility,
faith, hope, and love.

But the greatest of these is love.

FOR FURTHER READING

Allison, Lon and Anderson, Mark. *Going Public with the Gospel: Reviving Evangelistic Proclamation.* InterVarsity Press, 2004.

Brother Lawrence and Laubach, Frank. *Practicing His Presence.* The SeedSowers, 1973.

Collins, James C. *Good to Great: Why Some Companies Make the Leap ... and Others Don't.* HarperCollins Publishers, 2001.

Collins, James C., and Porras, Jerry I. *Built to Last: Successful Habits of Visionary Companies.* HarperCollins Publishers, 1994.

DePree, Max. *Leadership Jazz.* Dell Publishing/Bantam Doubleday Dell Publishing Group, 1993.

Drucker, Peter E. *The Effective Executive.* HarperCollins Publishers, 1967.

Eiseley, Loren. *The Star Thrower.* Harvest/HBJ, 1978.

Ford, Leighton. *Transforming Leadership: Jesus' Way of Creating Vision, Shaping Values and Empowering Change.* InterVarsity Press, 1991.

Graham, Billy. *A Biblical Standard for Evangelists.* WorldWide Publishing, 1984.

Footprints of Conscience. WorldWide Publishing, 1991.

Hope for the Troubled Heart. Word Publishing, 1991.

Just As I Am. HarperSanFrancisco/Zondervan, 1977.

Peace with God. Word Books and Worldwide Publications, 1984.

The Secret of Happiness. Word Publishing, 1985.

Griffin, William, and Dienert, Ruth Graham, compilers. *The Faithful Christian: An Anthology of Billy Graham.* McCracken Press, 1994.

Hybels, Bill. *Courageous Leadership.* Zondervan, 2002.

Lewis, C. S. *The Silver Chair—Book 4 in the Chronicles of Narnia.* Scholastic, Inc./Macmillan Publishing, 1987.

Loehr, James E. *Stress for Success.* Three Rivers Press/Random House, 1997.

Toughness Training for Life. Plume/Penguin Putnam, Inc., 1994.

MacDonald, Gordon. *The Life God Blesses.* Thomas Nelson Publishers, 1994.

Mid-Course Correction: Re-Ordering Your Private World for the Next Part of Your Journey. Thomas Nelson, Inc., 2000.

Martin, William. *A Prophet with Honor.* William Morrow and Company, 1991.

Maxwell, John C. *The 17 Indisputable Laws of Teamwork.* Thomas Nelson, 2001.

The 21 Indispensable Qualities of a Leader. Thomas Nelson, 1999.

Failing Forward: Turning Mistakes into Stepping Stones for Success. Thomas Nelson, 2000.

McLellan, Vernon K., compiler. *Billy Graham: A Tribute from Friends.* Warner Faith, 2002.

Pollard, C. William. *The Soul of the Firm.* Zondervan/HarperCollins, 1996.

Smith, Fred, Sr. *Leading with Integrity: Competence with Christian Character.* The Pastor's Soul Series, Bethany House Publishers, 1999.

Learning to Lead: Bringing Out the Best in People. The Leadership Library, Leadership/Word Books, 1986.

You and Your Network. Word Books, 1984.

Tada, Joni Eareckson. *The God I Love.* Zondervan, 2003.

Wilson, Grady. *Count It All Joy.* Grason/Broadman Press, 1984.

Wirt, Sherwood Eliot. *Billy: A Personal Look at Billy Graham, the World's Best-Loved Evangelist.* Crossway Books/Good News Publishers, 1997.

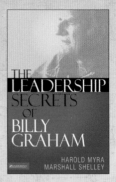

Now Available

ISBN 0-310-25578-3

US $24.99/UK £14.99/CAN $34.99

CHRISTIAN LIVING / PRACTICAL LIFE / BUSINESS & LEADERSHIP

At Inspirio, we love to hear from you—
your stories, your feedback,
and your product ideas.
Please send your comments to us
by way of email at
icares@zondervan.com
or to the address below:

inspirio

Attn: Inspirio Cares
5300 Patterson Avenue SE
Grand Rapids, MI 49530

If you would like further information
about Inspirio and the products we create,
please visit us at:
www.inspiriogifts.com

Thank you and God bless!